Global Stage

Language Book 3

Shelagh Speers

macmillan education

Scope and Sequence

Unit	Vocabulary	Explore Language	Global Citizenship
Language Review	**Vocabulary** *Nature, Weather, Food, Adjectives, Animals, Action Verbs* **Grammar** *Present Progressive, Comparative and Superlative Adjectives, Simple Past*		
1 I Love Reading page 10	**Books and Reading** *adventure, biography, boring, complicated, exciting, famous, fantasy, interesting, novel, popular, science fiction* **School Subjects** *art, English, geography, health, history, math, music, P.E. (physical education), science, technology* **Song** *The Library*	Simple Past: Regular and Irregular Verbs Adverbs of Manner	Why do communities need libraries? **Listening Skills** Listening for gist and details
2 What Lives Here? page 22	**The World Around Us** *biome, camel, cheetah, desert, dry, forest, grassland, plants, polar bear, tundra, wet, wolf* **Plants** *bud, flower, ground, leaves, petal, pollen, roots, seeds, shoot, stem* **Song** *Different Homes*	Comparatives and Superlatives: Short and Long Adjectives Comparatives and Superlatives: Short and Long Adverbs	How do plants grow in difficult climates? **Listening Skills** Listening for gist and details
Put It Together	Review Units 1 and 2 *Where in the World?*		
3 How Much Is It? page 36	**Money 1** *allowance, buy, cashier, customer, change, cheap, expensive, pay, save, sell, spend, wallet* **Money 2** *add, bills, dime, cents, coins, dollar, equals, nickel, penny, quarter, subtract* **Song** *Mone! Money! Money!*	Modal Verbs: *Have to* and *Don't Have to* Modal Verbs: *Should, Shouldn't,* and *Could*	What can people do with money? **Listening Skills** Listening for gist and details
4 We Can Do It page 48	**Performance** *actor, audience, backstage, costume, crew, curtain, director, nervous, performance, script, set, stage* **Time** *early, lasts, late, midnight, noon, on time, rehearsal, schedule, team* **Song** *Are You Ready?*	Past Progressive: Statements Past Progressive: Questions	How do performances bring people together? **Listening Skills** Listening for gist and details
Put It Together	Review Units 3 and 4 *Come to the Show!*		
5 Make Some Noise page 62	**Noises** *bang, bark, buzz, chirp, crash, crunch, splash, squeak, whisper, whistle* **Musical Instruments** *cello, clarinet, conductor, drums, flute, harp, orchestra, piano, trumpet, violin, xylophone* **Song** *Are You Awake?*	Future Plans: *Going to* Statements Future Plans: *Going to* Questions	Why are there different kinds of music? **Listening Skills** Listening for gist and details

Speaking	Writing	International English	Literacy Book
			Literacy Review: Scanning; Cause and Effect; Sequence of Events; Main Idea and Details; Fact and Opinion; *st; tr; nd; ng*
Conversation Asking for and offering help and advice **Pronunciation** /sk / and /gr/	**Word Building** Adverb endings **Product** A Book Report		**Fantasy** *The Beginning of Alice's Adventures* **Informational Text** *Learning and Your Brain* **Reading Skill** Skimming a text
Presentation Describing biomes **Pronunciation** /pl/ and /kl/	**Sentence Building** Sequencers **Product** Writing Instructions	**US** *plastic wrap* **UK** *cling film*	**Informational Text** *Two Different Forests* **Folk Tale** *A New Friend* **Reading Skill** Understanding the author's purpose
Conversation Buying a birthday present **Pronunciation** /pr/ and /dr/	**Sentence Building** Conjunctions: *and, but, so* **Product** Anecdotal Paragraph	**US** *allowance; bill; college* **UK** *pocket money; note; university*	**Informational Text** *The History of Money* **Story** *The $100 Bill* **Reading Skill** Identifying problems and solutions
Presentation Describing a hobby **Pronunciation** /ð/ and /θ/	**Sentence Building** Time phrases and commas **Product** A Diary Entry		**Informational Text** *Teamwork Makes the Dream Work* **Play** *Late for the Show* **Reading Skill** Understanding the sequence of events
Conversation Agreeing and disagreeing **Pronunciation** /θ/ and /ʧ/	**Punctuation** Using quotation marks and commas **Product** A Description	**US** *program; have a show; apartment* **UK** *programme; do a show; flat*	**Informational Text** *The Art of Sound* **Poem** *Beethoven's 9th* **Reading Skill** Understanding cause and effect

Speaking	Writing	International English	Literacy Book
Conversation Talking about a menu **Pronunciation** /fr/ and /bl/	**Text Features** Using Headings **Product** Describing an Experiment	**US** *trash can; server* **UK** *rubbish bin; waiter/waitress*	**Story** *Little Chef* **Persuasive Text** *Too Young to Cook? True Stories of Young Chefs* **Reading Skill** Scanning for specific information
Presentation Describing a dream job **Pronunciation** /str/ and /tr/	**Punctuation** Using exclamation points and quotation marks **Product** Finishing a Story	**US** *fire truck; truck; student; named; exclamation point* **UK** *fire engine; lorry; pupil; called; exclamation mark*	**Story** *What Happens Next?* **Informational Text** *Animals to the Rescue* **Reading Skill** Making inferences and predictions
Presentation An endangered animal **Pronunciation** /h/ and /w/	**Word Building** Synonyms **Product** A Concrete Poem	**US** *ocean floor* **UK** *seabed*	**Persuasive Text** *Coral Reefs* **Fantasy** *The Lost Camera* **Reading Skill** Identifying perspective
Conversation Giving health advice **Pronunciation** /kw/ and /kr/	**Spelling** Simple past irregular verb forms **Product** A Letter to a Friend	**US** *have a fever, sick; clinic, shot* **UK** *have a temperature, ill; health centre, injection*	**Informational Text** *Take Your Medicine* **Story** *A Surprise Cure* **Reading Skill** Understanding main ideas and details
Presentation Telling a story about something you made **Pronunciation** /br/ and /fl/	**Paragraph Building** Transition: words and phrases **Product** A Story		**Informational Text** *Moving Machines* **Science Fiction** *Searching for Sterling* **Reading Skill** Understanding facts and opinions

A Listen and write. What's beautiful?

1 unsmoatin ____________

2 wson ____________

3 laltwreaf ____________

4 tefsor ____________

5 elak ____________

6 bcahe ____________

7 arin ____________

8 noriwba ____________

B Look and write.

Across

1 

6 

7 

8 

Down

2 

3 

4 

5 

6 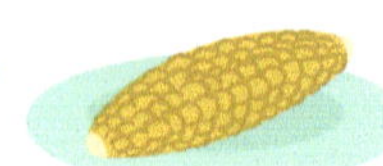

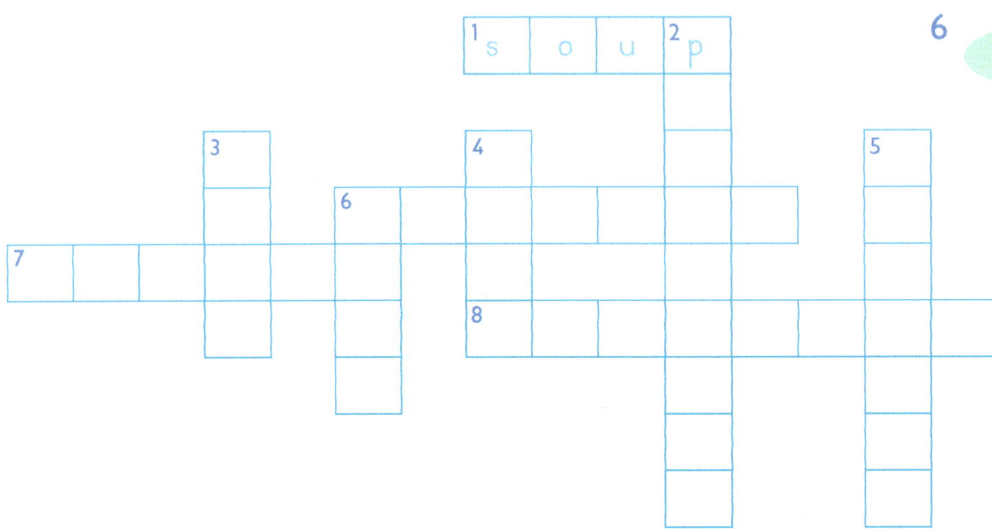

C Look and match. Then complete. Use the words in the boxes.

chameleon penguin dinosaur duck ~~snake~~ bear

dangerous soft huge dirty tiny slow

1 Be careful! That snake is ______________ .

2 That ______________ is ______________ . It's so big!

3 That ______________ is ______________ and it has a fish!

4 Look at the ______________ in my hand. It's ______________ !

5 The little ______________ is very ______________ .

6 The ______________ has ______________ feathers.

D Find the verbs. Then choose four and make sentences with a partner.

1 ______________

2 ______________

3 ______________

4 ______________

A Look and complete. What are they doing?

B Listen and complete.

Ted: Look at those boats! There's a kayak and a sailboat.

Sadie: The sailboat is 1 faster (fast) than the kayak.

Jeff: Yes. The kayak is 2 ______ (slow), and it's also 3 ______ (small).

Sadie: I think sailing is 4 ______ (exciting) than kayaking.

Ted: I went sailing and kayaking with my cousin last summer. Sailing was 5 ______ (difficult) than kayaking!

Jeff: Really? Why?

Ted: I needed help. I was strong, but my cousin was 6 ______ (strong)!

Sadie: So, kayaking was 7 ______ (good) for you?

Ted: Yes. I really liked it. It was 8 ______ (quiet) and ______ (interesting). And I did it by myself!

C Read and complete.

Today it's sunny at the lake, but yesterday there 1 was (be) a lot of rain. I 2 ________ (see) lightning in the sky, but I 3 ________ (not be) frightened of the thunder. I 4 ________ (play) with my brothers all day. We 5 ________ (run) around our house, and we 6 ________ (be) very noisy. Finally, we 7 ________ (eat) dinner and 8 ________ (go) to bed. Today's a better day!

D Look at A. Complete.

small ~~big~~ curly straight beautiful bad long

1 Ted's backpack is the biggest .
2 Sadie's lunch is ________.
3 Jeff's painting is ________.
4 Sadie's hair is ________.
5 Jeff's hair is ________.
6 Ted's painting is ________.

UNIT 1 I Love Reading

A Listen and find. Who gets books for Kareem?

B Listen, say, and number the pictures in A.

C Close your eyes. Listen, visualize, and say.

D Look and write.

Kinds of books	How to describe books
novels	interesting

E Listen and complete. Then watch and sing.

The Library

There's a world of information for you and me—everything you want at the library.
Books, games, computers, and movies you can see. There's a lot to learn and do at the library!

You can sit and read a **1** n o v e l at the library
Go on an **2** a __ v __ __ tu __ e through the pictures you see
You can find **3** e __ __ i t __ __ __ stories or a **4** f __ __ __ a __ y
The library's never **5** bo __ __ __ g, and it's all free!

You can listen to great music at the library
And find a **6** f __ __ o __ s person's **7** b __ __ g r __ p __ __
You can meet **8** i __ __ __ r e __ __ __ n __ people—maybe two or three
The library's very popular, and it's all free!

Explore Language

A Listen and read. What's Gavin's project about?

1

Gavin: Where did you go yesterday after school, Kareem?

Kareem: I went to the library with my project group.

Gavin: What did you do there?

Kareem: We looked for books about robots.

Gavin: Did you find anything?

Kareem: Yes, we did. We read about the very first robot.

Gavin: Cool! I worked on my project, too.

Kareem: I didn't see you there, Gavin.

Gavin: Oh, I didn't go to the library.

Kareem: Where did you go?

Gavin: My project's about frogs, so I went to the river. And I found this!

2

B Look at **A**. Complete.

Simple Past

Where	**did**	you	______	yesterday after school?
I	______			to the library with my project group.
We	______	for		books about robots.

______	you	______	anything?	Yes, we ______ .	No, we **didn't**.

Watch Out

I read = simple present
I read = simple past

C Think and discuss. Then choose.

1 We use the simple past to talk about now / before now.

D Listen and say.

E Help Millie write in her diary. Look and complete.

1 Yesterday, I went (go) to the library. 2 I ______ (look) for an interesting novel. 3 I ______ (not want) a complicated story. 4 I ______ (not see) any of my friends there. 5 I ______ (find) lots of nonfiction books. 6 I ______ (borrow) two biographies of famous people.

F Play a chain game. Talk about yesterday.

Yesterday, I went kayaking after school.

Yesterday, she went kayaking, and I read a comic book.

Yesterday, she went kayaking, he read a comic book, and I found a frog.

Why do communities need libraries?

A Listen to Linda talk about her library. How does it grow?

- geography ☐
- science 1
- music ☐
- technology ☐
- P.E. (physical education) ☐
- math ☐
- history ☐
- art ☐
- health ☐
- English ☐

B Listen, say, and number the pictures in **A**.

C Read and complete.

1 My brother likes _history_ because he thinks the past is interesting.

2 We learn about other countries and people in __________ .

3 I like __________ the best because we can play games outside.

4 __________ is my favorite subject because we read good stories.

5 I love __________ because I want to know all about animals and plants.

6 In __________ class, we learn how to take care of ourselves.

D *Now listen to Skyla and Rishi. Why do these libraries travel to different places?*

Skyla, the Netherlands

Rishi, India

E Listen again. Check (✔) the correct country.

Which country's library ...	India	The Netherlands
1 goes to schools?	◯	✔
2 stops in small towns and villages?	◯	◯
3 has places to read?	◯	◯
4 travels for hours?	◯	◯
5 has books in many languages?	◯	◯

What things can you do at your library?
How can we share books in our communities?

A Listen and read. What did Lena learn about penguins?

1

Millie: Is that a science book, Lena?

Lena: Yes, it's all about animals.

Millie: Cool! I just read a book about penguins yesterday.

Lena: You read a whole book in one day? That was quick!

Millie: Well, I read quickly.

Lena: I don't. I read very slowly.

2

Millie: Why?

Lena: So I can remember every word.

Millie: Can you really remember *everything*? What's the first sentence?

Lena: "Penguins are birds, but they can't fly."

Millie: Wow, you really do read carefully!

B Look at A. Complete.

Adverbs of Manner

Adjectives					Adverbs		
I	'm	a	quick	reader.	I	read	________ .
			slow				________ .
You	're		careful		You	really do read	________ .

quick + –ly = quickly
easy + –ly = easily

Remember

C Think and discuss. Then choose.

1 We use an adverb / adjective to describe a noun.

2 We use an adverb / adjective to describe a verb.

3 We use adverbs of manner to describe how / when an action happens.

D Listen and say.

E Read and choose.

1 The girls talk quiet / quietly in the library.

2 We're late because the school bus is going slow / slowly.

3 That's an easy / easily book. It has a lot of pictures.

4 He read the instructions careful / carefully. They were complicated.

5 The boys finished the test quick / quickly. They knew the answers.

6 I was happy / happily in my art class.

F Choose and say. Make sentences about you, your family, and friends.

eat sing read write
shout cry run walk

quickly carefully loudly
easily quietly slowly noisily

My little sister eats quickly.

My friend Bassem walks slowly.

A Watch and listen. Which book does Rania choose?

Watch
Do the girls look at each other or at the books when they speak?

B Watch again. Check (✔) the phrases you hear.

1 ✔ Why don't you get this book?
2 ◯ What kind of book is it?
3 ◯ It sounds great.
4 ◯ How about this book?
5 ◯ What books do you have?
6 ◯ What's it about?
7 ◯ It doesn't sound very interesting.
8 ◯ What happens?
9 ◯ OK, let's get it.

Pronunciation /sk/ and /gr/

Listen and say.

ask scary school great grows agree

What other words do you know with these sounds?

C Plan. Think about two books to recommend. Complete.

Book 1	Book 2
Title:	Title:
Kind of book:	Kind of book:
Main character:	Main character:
What happens:	What happens:

D Prepare your conversation. Use your ideas from C and the phrases from B.

read

A

Make a suggestion
What do you think of ...

B

Ask for more information
What kind of ...

A

Give a description

B

Give your opinion

A

Agree or disagree

B

Make a decision

E Practice with a friend.

Reflect
Did I look at my friend?
Yes / No

Write About It

A Read the book report. Underline the adverbs of manner.

Name: Ana Sánchez
Title: Fantastic Mr. Fox
Author: Roald Dahl

Who are the main characters?
Farmer Boggis, Farmer Bunce, Farmer Bean, Mr. Fox

What happens in the book?
The farmers don't like Mr. Fox. They shout at him angrily because he takes their food. They try to catch him, but he escapes easily. Mr. Fox is smart!

Did you like this book? Why or why not?
This book is very good! I read it quickly. I liked it because it is funny. Also, I really liked the animal characters. I give this book five stars!

My favorite part: ★★★★★

B Change the adjectives into adverbs. Complete.

~~angry~~ ~~careful~~ clever easy happy loud quiet quick sad slow

~~y~~ + –ily	angrily		
+ –ly	carefully		

C Think about a book you read. Complete the story map.

Title:	Main Characters:	What Happens:	Did I like it? Why or why not?
Author:			

D Write your book report.

Reflect
Did I use adverbs of manner?

Read the questions and draw or write your answers.

What did I do?

What did I learn?

How did I learn?

How well did I do?

Hello! I'm Millie. Where do I go next?
Find out in Unit 2!

What can I do next?

- Sing
- Find out more
- Share
- Talk

UNIT 2

What Lives Here?

A Listen and find. Which four biomes do the girls see?

B Listen, say, and number the pictures in **A**.

C Close your eyes. Listen, visualize, and say.

D Look and write.

Biomes	Animals	Climate
forest		hot
		cold

E Listen and complete. Then watch and sing.

Different Homes

Where on Earth do you live? Where on Earth is your home?
The climate, plants, and animals make your biome your home.

The 1 desert is hot and dry
Not much can grow on the land
But the 2 c__________ walks through the sand.

The 3 t__________ has no trees
It's cold but small flowers grow
And the 4 p__________ plays in the snow.

The 5 g__________ has tall, tall grass
It's dry and the wind is strong
And the 6 c__________ runs all day long.

The 7 f__________ is full of green trees
The sun shines warm and bright
But the 8 w__________ sleeps until night.

Explore Language

A Listen and read. Which animals do the girls talk about?

1

2

3

Tess: The elephant? Are elephants dangerous?

Ava: Yes, some people say elephants are more dangerous than lions. They say elephants are the most dangerous animals of all!

B Look at **A**. Complete.

Comparative and Superlative Adjectives

This lion	's	bigger			the cheetah.
Elephants	are	______	______	______	lions.

Is	the lion	______	______	animal in the grassland?
Elephants	are	___ ___	______	animals of all!

good → better → the best
bad → worse → the worst

Remember

C Think and discuss. Then choose.

1. We use comparative / superlative adjectives to compare two things.
2. We use comparative / superlative adjectives to compare three or more things.

D Listen and say.

E Read and complete.

1. The sand in the desert is the softest (soft) in the world.
2. The tundra is ______________________ (cold) the forest.
3. I like this climate ______________________ (good) the desert climate.
4. The flowers in the forest are ______________________ (beautiful) than these.
5. The grassland is ______________________ (good) place for cheetahs.
6. I think the grassland is the ______________________ (interesting) biome.

F Make sentences about biomes. Choose and say.

hot   cold   wet   dry   interesting   beautiful

The tundra is the most interesting because it has lots of animals.

The grassland is colder than the desert.

How do plants grow in difficult climates?

A Listen to Iqaluk talk about a flower on the tundra. What color is it?

B Listen, say, and number the pictures in **A**.

C Look and complete.

1 flower

2 ______

3 ______

4 ______

5 ______

6 ______

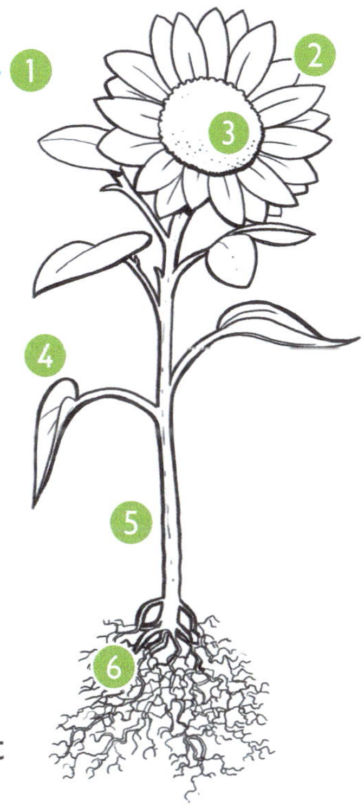

D Now listen to Amadou and Seba. Which plant grows in the water?

Amadou, Senegal

Seba, Egypt

E Listen again. Write *True* or *False*.

1 The baoab tree only grows in Senegal. False

2 It's a small tree. ______

3 The tree is called the "tree of life". ______

4 The blue water lily grows in Senegal. ______

5 The blue water lily is one of the oldest flowers. ______

What plants or flowers grow in your country? How can people help plants or flowers grow?

Explore Language

A Listen and read. What happened to Ava?

Grammar Comparatives and Superlatives: Short and Long Adverbs

B Look at **A**. Complete.

Comparative Adverbs

It	grows	______	______	______	the plant next to it.

Superlative Adverbs

Desert plants	grow	______	______	______	of all.

Always use *than* with the comparative.
Always use *the* with the superlative.

Remember

C Think and discuss. Then choose.

1. We use comparative / superlative adverbs to compare two actions.
2. We use comparative / superlative adverbs to compare three or more actions.

D Listen and say.

E Read and complete.

1. Flowers grow in the forest more easily than (easy) in the desert.
2. In hot weather, I walk ______________________ (slow) in cold weather.
3. Plants in the forest grow ______________________ (quick) of all.
4. We take care of flowers ______________________ (careful) trees.
5. I can grow this plant from a seed ______________________ (easy) of all.
6. The roots grow in wet ground ______________________ (quick) in dry ground.

F Make sentences comparing how your classmates do things. Do you agree or disagree?

In Our Class
Nate writes the most carefully.
Sunita writes less carefully than Nate.

I disagree! Sunita writes more carefully than Nate.

Nate writes the most carefully in our class.

Take the Stage

A Watch and listen. Would you like to live in Rania's biome?

Watch
What does she do when she talks about something on her poster?

B Watch again. Check (✔) the phrases you hear.

1. ✔ I'm going to talk about its climate, plants, and animals.
2. ◯ Let me tell you about the sun forest.
3. ◯ The climate is hot and wet.
4. ◯ The plants are tall and green.
5. ◯ One special plant is the super-sunflower.
6. ◯ All the animals sleep in the trees at night.
7. ◯ One special animal is the *sunkey*.
8. ◯ I like my biome best because it's the sunniest place of all.

Pronunciation /pl/ and /kl/

Listen and say.

plants play place climate clouds close

What other words do you know with these sounds?

C Plan. Think about your dream biome. Write.

Climate

Plants

Animals

D Prepare your presentation. Use your ideas from **C** and phrases from **B**.

Introduction

This is my dream biome ...

Middle

The climate is ...

Ending

My dream biome is the best because ...

E Practice with a friend. Then share with your class.

Reflect

Did I point to my poster and look at the audience?

Yes / No

Write About It

A Read the instructions. Circle the sequencers and underline the imperatives.

What you need: a jar, a bean, water, two paper towels, plastic wrap

How To Grow A Bean Plant

Before you start, make a list. Then, find everything.
First, put the paper towels in water and take them out.
Next, put one wet paper towel in the jar.
Then, put the bean on the paper towel and put the other paper towel over it.
After that, cover the jar with plastic wrap and cut a small hole in it. Don't make the hole too big!
Finally, put the jar near a sunny window. Watch your bean shoot grow.

plastic wrap | cling film

B Add sequencers and change the sentences into imperatives. Write.

~~First~~ Finally After that Next Then

1 You make a list. First, make a list.

2 You look for everything you need. __________

3 You put one wet paper towel in the jar. __________

4 You put the seed in the jar. __________

5 You find a sunny place for the jar. __________

C Plan. Complete the steps to grow a pumpkin.

What I need:	Steps:
	1 __________
	2 __________
	3 __________
	4 __________

Reflect
Did I use sequencers correctly?

D Write your instructions. Make a poster and add pictures.

Read the questions and draw or write your answers.

What did I do?

What did I learn?

What was my favorite part?

How well did I do?

What can I do next?

- Read
- Practice
- Write
- Listen

Hello! I'm Owen. What store do I go to? Find out in Unit 3.

UNIT 1
UNIT 2

Where in the World?

Tundra

the most exciting

Did you do your math homework last night?

grassland
tundra

The (grassland) is warmer than the (tundra).

You did it! Color the roots.

biography
novel

HOW TO PLAY

1 Play in teams of four. Each player chooses one biome to start.

2 Take turns visiting each square in your biomes. Answer the questions or make a comparison using the words or images.

3 When you finish your biome, color in a part of the plant.

4 The first team to color the whole plant is the winner.

I think (technology) is the most complicated (subject).

Forest

Who's the funniest person in your class?

the most complicated

English
geography

Where did you go last weekend?

Congratulations! Color the petals.

history
music

Who's the most famous person in the world?

the most interesting

desert
forest

Desert

Nice job! Color the stem.

This grass is (greener) than that grass.

Grassland

Where did you go last weekend?

What climate do you like best?

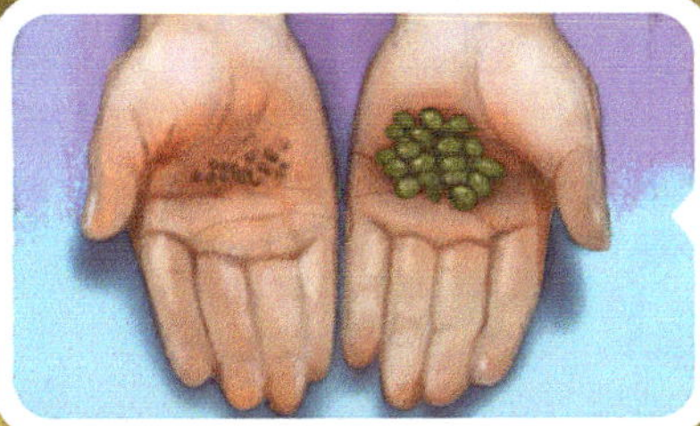

What's the most popular book in your class?

wolf
cheetah

Excellent! Color the leaves.

I like the (grassland) the best!

UNIT 3 How Much Is It?

A Listen and find. How much does the shirt cost?

🇺🇸	🇬🇧
allowance	pocket money

B Listen, say, and number the pictures in **A**.

C Close your eyes. Listen, visualize, and say.

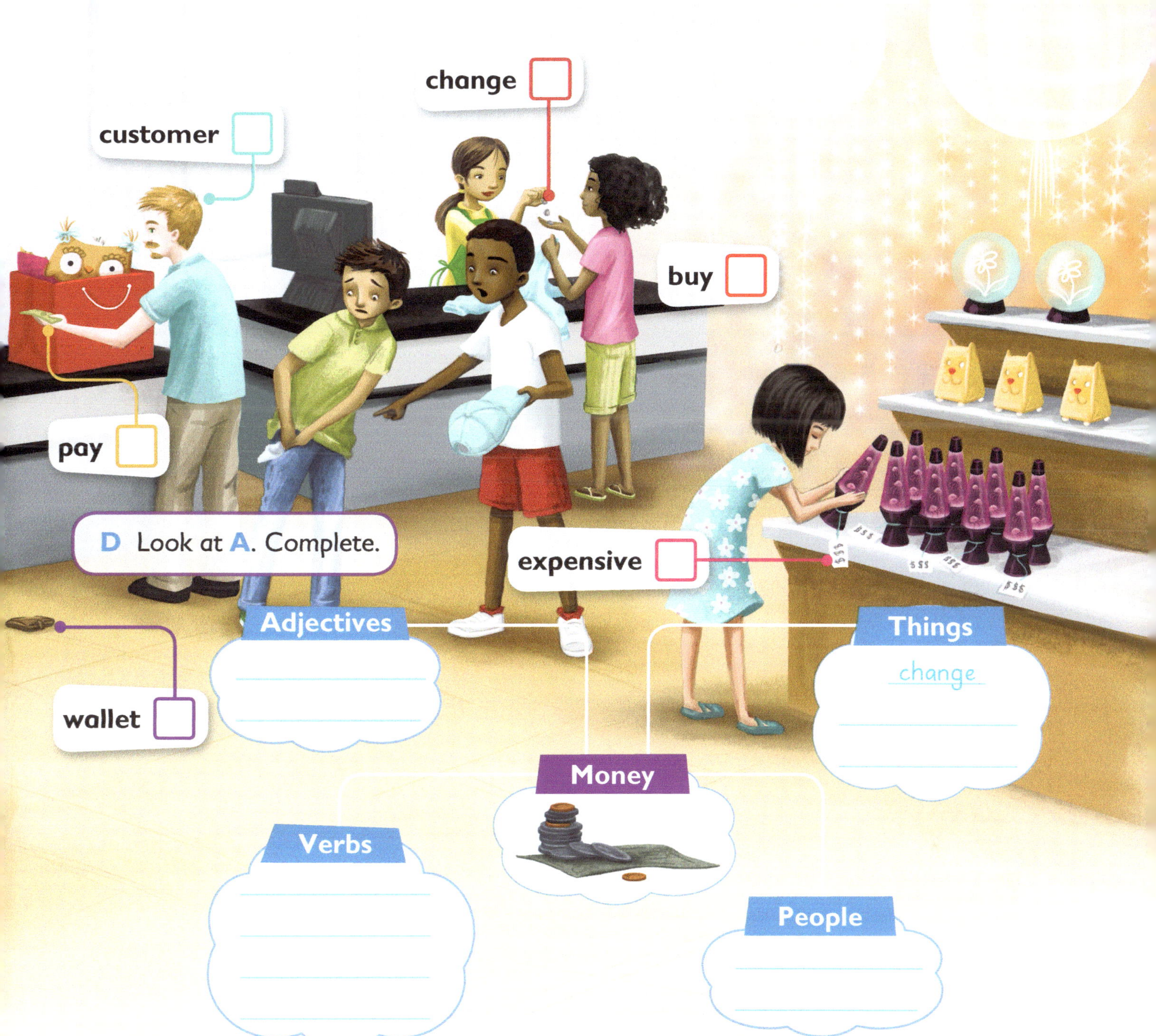

D Look at **A**. Complete.

E Listen and complete. Then watch and sing.

Money! Money! Money!

Money! Money! Money! We **1** spend (psedn) some every day
We take our **2** __________ (llstwae) to the store, we **3** __________ (uyb) things, and we pay!

Toys! Snacks! Video games! Lunch! Drinks! Ice cream!

Money! Money! Money! We get some every day
The **4** __________ (omcuertss) come to our store, we **5** __________ (elsl) things, and they pay!

Money! Money! Money! We **6** __________ (avse) some every day
We count our money carefully and put it all away! YAY!

Explore Language

A Listen and read. How does Owen get his money?

1

Charlie: Let's get a snack.
Owen: I can't. I spent all my money.
Charlie: I have some. Do your parents give you money often?
Owen: Well, I get an allowance, but I have to help at home.
Charlie: Oh, really? What do you have to do?

2

Owen: I have to make my bed and wash the dishes. What about you?
Charlie: I have to clean my room and help with dinner, but I don't get an allowance.

3

Owen: Do you have to make your bed?
Charlie: Yes, I do. But I don't have to wash the dishes.
Owen: Why not?
Charlie: Because we have a dishwasher!

4

B Look at **A**. Complete.

Have to and Don't Have to

What	do	you	have to	do?	
I	______	clean my room.	I	______	wash the dishes.
He	has to	wash the car.	He	doesn't have to	clean the table.

______	you	______	make your bed?	Yes, I ______ .	No, I don't.

Watch Out

Yes, I do. not ~~*Yes, I have.*~~
No, I don't. not ~~*No, I haven't.*~~

C Think and discuss. Then choose.

1 We use *have to* + verb when we need to / don't need to do something.

2 We use *don't have to* + verb when we need to / don't need to do something.

D Listen and say.

E Look, read, and complete.

~~clean~~ help finish clean wash

1 She has to clean the floor, but he ______ .

2 They ______ their homework.

3 He ______ the dishes.

4 They ______ the table.

5 ______ she ______ him?

F Play *Find Someone Who*. Write three sentences about jobs you have to do at home.

1 I have to wash the dishes.

2

3

I have to wash the dishes. What about you?

I don't have to wash the dishes. But I have to clean my room. Do you?

What can people do with money?

A Listen to Annette talk about her American coins. Why does Sumiko like coins?

penny [1]

nickel [ ]

dime [ ]

quarter [ ]

dollar [ ]

bills [ ]

equals [ ]

add [ ]

cents [ ]

coins [ ]

subtract [ ]

B Listen, say, and number the pictures in A.

C Read and complete.

1 A penny is one cent. A ________ is five ________ . A ________ is ten cents.

2 Four ________ is one ________ .

3 You can spend dollar ________ or dollar ________ .

4 ________ a quarter and a nickel. How much do you have? ________ cents

5 ________ a dime from a dollar. How much do you have? ________ cents

6 $1.25 ________ one dollar and twenty-five cents.

D Now listen to Leena and Davi. Why does Leena save her coins?

Leena, Jordan

Davi, Brazil

E Listen again. Check (✔) the correct person.

Who …	Leena	Davi
1 helps other people?	○	✔
2 collected coins at school?	○	○
3 brings coins to the bank?	○	○
4 gives away coins?	○	○
5 saves coins for college?	○	○

college (US) / university (UK)

What do you do with coins?
How can we use coins to help our communities?

Explore Language

A Listen and read. How much money does Andie spend?

1

Ting: Andie, should I buy this lamp? It's $25. That's all my money.

Andie: You shouldn't spend it all on a lamp, Ting. You should save some money for later.

Ting: I know, but it's so cool. Look at the colors!

Andie: You could buy these lights. They're only $10.

2

Ting: I could, but …

Andie: You could even buy two sets of lights!

Ting: Yes, but …

Andie: You know, maybe you *should* buy the lamp. You love it. I'm going to buy a set of these lights for my room!

3

B Look at **A**. Complete.

Should, Shouldn't, and Could

You	should	buy	the lamp.	You	______	spend	it all on a lamp.
	______		these lights.		______	save	some money.
______	I	buy this lamp?		Yes, you ______ .		No, you ______ .	

Remember

Should and *could* rhyme with *good*.

C Think and discuss. Then choose.

1 We use *should* / *could* to give advice.

2 We use *should* / *could* to give choices.

D Listen and say.

E Complete the sentences with *could* or *should*.

1 These chips are $1.00. I <u>could</u> pay with a dollar bill or four quarters.

2 You ______ buy some water. You look so thirsty!

3 We found $5.00 on the playground. ______ we give it to our teacher?

4 My brother got some money for his birthday. He ______ spend it now or save it for later!

5 Our class is saving money for a trip. We ______ sell cookies or we ______ wash cars.

6 You ______ always count your change carefully.

F Play *What to Do?* Read, think, and discuss.

You each have three dollars. You want to buy a snack. You also have to take the bus home. The bus costs $1.75 each.

What could you buy? What should you do? How many ways can you spend the money?

We could both buy potato chips.

Or we could buy two sandwiches and walk home.

Talk About It

A Watch and listen. What present does Anya buy?

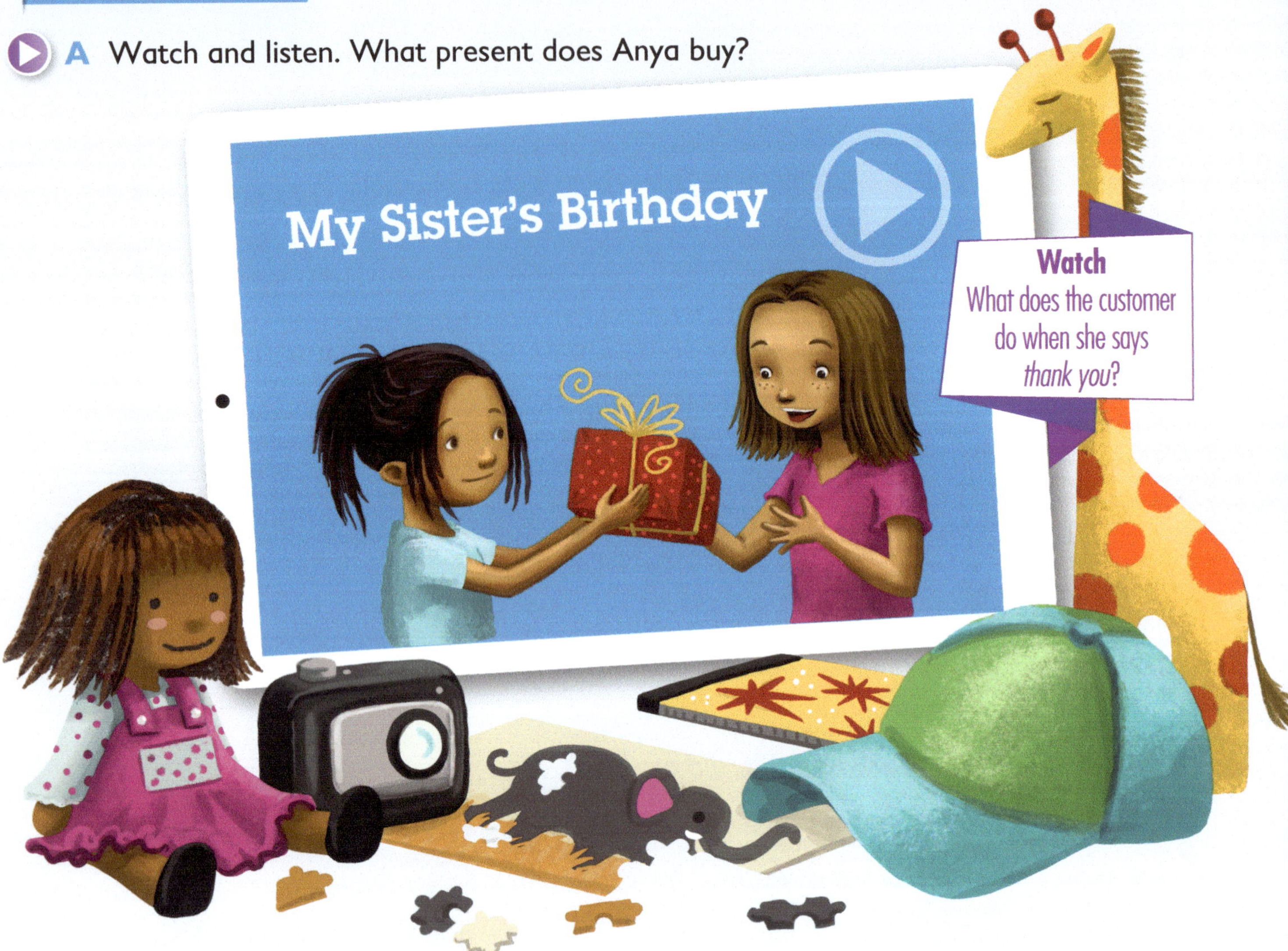

B Watch again. Check (✔) the phrases you hear.

1 ✔ Can I help you?
2 ◯ I'm looking for a present for my mom.
3 ◯ She likes games and puzzles.
4 ◯ You could get her this lamp.
5 ◯ I think you should buy her the video game.
6 ◯ Good choice!
7 ◯ Thank you very much.
8 ◯ Have a nice day!

Pronunciation /pr/ and /dr/

Listen and say.

present pretty surprised drinks draw drive

What other words do you know with these sounds?

C Plan. Choose two people. Think about buying them a present. Check (✔) and write.

- mom ◯
- grandpa ◯
- friend ◯
- ______ ◯

flowers	socks
board game	book
teddy bear	puzzle
______	
______	

1 Person: ______ Present: ______

2 Person: ______ Present: ______

D Prepare your conversation. Use your ideas from **C** and phrases from **B**.

A **Say hello and offer to help**

Hi! Can I ...

B **Say who the present is for**

______

A **Make a suggestion**

______

B **Say what the person likes**

______

A **Make another suggestion**

______

B **Make a decision**

______

Reflect

Did I look at my partner and smile?

Yes / No

E Practice with a friend.

Write About It

A Read the paragraph. Underline *and*, *but*, and *so*. Circle the punctuation that comes before these words.

My Paddle Board

Last summer, I went paddle boarding at the lake, and it was fun! At first, I fell in the water, but I quickly learned to stand. After that, I wanted one of my own, so I saved my money all year. People gave me money as a gift for my birthday, and I saved it in a box. I also saved my allowance from my mom and dad. I have to help at home to get it. Every week, I have to clean my room, and every day I have to wash the dishes. After a year, I counted my money. My dad took me to the store, and I finally bought my paddle board. It's beautiful!

B Look at A. Match.

1 I wanted a paddle board, so
2 I saved my birthday money, and
3 I got money for my birthday, but
4 I have to wash the dishes, and
5 I fell off the paddle board at first, but

a. I didn't spend it.
b. I have to clean my room, too.
c. I saved my money for a year.
d. I quickly learned to stand on it.
e. I also saved money from my mom and dad.

C Plan. Think about something you saved money for. Answer the questions.

1 What was it? ______
2 How did you save money? ______
3 How long did you save money for? ______
4 Where did you put the money? ______
5 What happened? ______

Reflect
Did I use *and*, *but*, and *so*?

D Write your paragraph. Find or draw a picture to go with it.

Read the questions and draw or write your answers.

What did I do?

How did I learn?

What did I learn?

How well did I do?

What can I do next?

Hello! I'm Ting. What will I perform? Find out in Unit 4.

UNIT 4

We Can Do It

A Listen and find. What time does the curtain open?

B Listen, say, and number the pictures in A.

C Close your eyes. Listen, visualize, and say.

D Look at **A**. Complete.

Who?	What?	Where?
	performance	
		How?

E Listen and complete. Then watch and sing.

Are You Ready?

Are you ready? We're ready! We're ready to perform!

We're 1 backstage and feeling 2 n ___ ___ v ___ us
We're going on 3 s ___ ___ g ___ soon. The play begins at eight.
We're behind the 4 cu ___ ___ a ___ ___ in our 5 c ___ s ___ u ___ ___ ___, and we look great!

We practiced hard and learned the 6 s ___ r ___ ___ t
We listened to our 7 d ___ ___ ___ c ___ ___ ___ and painted all the 8 s ___ ___ s
We hope no one forgets!

Explore Language

A Listen and read. Where was Fred?

Zora: Oh, no! What happened to the lights? Fred? Where are you? I can't see! Fred?

OK, let me think. At seven o'clock … Fred was standing by the curtain. Tommy and Ting were practicing the script. Nasir was checking the set.

The director was saying, "Places, everyone!" The actors weren't performing on stage. And it wasn't raining!

Zora: Oh good! There's Tommy, and Ting, and Nasir! But where's Fred?

Fred: Here I am! I was getting a candle.

B Look at **A**. Complete.

Past Progressive: Statements

Fred	______	______	by the curtain.	The actors	______	______	on stage.
Tommy and Ting	were	______	the script.	It	wasn't	______ !	

> A time phrase can come at the beginning or the end of the sentence.
>
> **Remember**

C Think and discuss. Then choose.

1 We use the past progressive to talk about actions that were happening in the past / future.

D Listen and say.

E Put the words in order.

1 at 4:00 / were / The / practicing / actors / the / play
The actors were practicing the play at 4:00.

2 finishing / The / crew / was / the / at 5:30. / set
____

3 we / backstage. / waiting / At 6:00, / weren't
____

4 was / at 7:00. / opening / curtain / The
____

5 the / watching / parents / were / at 8:00. / My / performance
____

6 the / At 8:30, / clapping. / audience / was
____

F Play a chain game. Choose a time. Make sentences about yesterday.

I was eating dinner at 7:30.

I wasn't eating dinner at 7:30. I was watching TV at 7:30.

I wasn't eating dinner or watching TV at 7:30. At 7:30, I was doing my homework.

How do performances bring people together?

A Listen to the interview. What important thing did the performers learn?

rehearsal ☐

team ☐

early ☐

on time ☐

late 1

schedule ☐

noon ☐

midnight ☐

lasts ☐

B Listen, say, and number the pictures in **A**.

C Read and complete.

1 Hundreds of children from my school danced in a _team_ in the Olympic Opening Ceremony.

2 We had a very busy __________ with __________ every day after school.

3 Our Saturday rehearsals start at ________ and end at __________. They __________ twelve hours!

4 Our director said, "Never be ________! Try to be ________. Always be __________."

D Now listen to Li Min and Adam. How did Li Min feel?

Li Min, China

Adam, UK

E Listen again. Choose.

1 Li Min helped to carry a (flag) / team in her performance.

2 She was wearing a beautiful Chinese / British costume.

3 Li Min's group practiced many / a few times.

4 Adam and the other children were water / flags in the river.

5 His costume / song was blue like water.

6 Adam's family was on stage / watching, but they didn't see him.

Would you like to be in a big performance?
When are there performances in your community?

Explore Language

A Listen and read. Why did the set fall down at the dance rehearsal?

Mr. Gates: Wow! What happened here?

Riya: Sorry, Mr. Gates. We were practicing our dance.

Marcus: And suddenly the set fell down.

Mr. Gates: What were you doing?

Ting: We were dancing!

Mr. Gates: Were you dancing over there?

Group: No, we weren't!

Mr. Gates: Who was watching the dance?

Jake: I was. I'm in the crew. I was finishing the lights.

Mr. Gates: Did you see anything?

Jake: Yes! A cat was climbing up the set.

Mr. Gates: A white cat?

Jake: Yes, and then all the boxes fell down.

Mr. Gates: Muffin! There you are. OK, kids. Let's fix the set!

B Look at **A**. Complete.

Past Progressive: Questions

What	were	you		________ ?	
______	you	________	over there?	Yes, we ________ .	No, we ________ .
Who	______	________	the dance?	I ________ .	We ________ .

C Think and discuss. Then choose.

1 Past progressive questions ask about something which happened during a period of time / at one time in the past.

Use *was/were* with *past progressive*, not ~~*does/did*~~.

Watch Out

D Listen and say.

E Complete the questions and answers.

1 What was he doing (do) at 6:00 yesterday evening?

He was putting on (put on) his costume.

2 ________ you ________ (eat) lunch at noon yesterday?

No, I ________ . I was going to my rehearsal.

3 Who ________ the director ________ (watch) during the rehearsal?

He ________ Ali.

4 What ________ the dancers ________ (think) about during the performance?

They ________ about the dance.

5 ________ she ________ (feel) proud after the performance? Yes, she ________ .

F Play *Find Someone Who*. Write three sentences about this morning. Use time phrases. Then talk to your friends.

1 At 5:30, I was sleeping.

2

3

What were you doing at 5:30?

I was sleeping!

Me, too!

Take the Stage

A Watch and listen. What does Natalia like about performing?

Watch
How does she get the audience's attention at the beginning?

B Watch again. Check (✔) the phrases you hear.

1. ✔ Today I'm going to talk about folk dancing.
2. ◯ I started dancing when I was five.
3. ◯ I go to dance class once a week.
4. ◯ I practice every day at home.
5. ◯ There are three things I like about performing.
6. ◯ The next thing I like is the teamwork.
7. ◯ And, finally, I like the audience.
8. ◯ Come and see me dance.

Pronunciation /ð/ and /θ/

Listen and say.

there they then think three things

What other words do you know with these sounds?

C Plan. Check (✔) the kinds of performances you do at or after school. Then choose one and complete.

◯ Dancing ◯ Acting ◯ Sports ◯ ______

Performance	
Do you take lessons?	Yes / No
Do you wear a costume or uniform?	Yes / No
When did you start?	
How often do you practice?	
What are three reasons you like it?	1
	2
	3
When's your next performance?	

D Prepare your presentation. Choose a performance from **C** and use phrases from **B**. Complete your note cards.

Introduction

Today, I'm going to talk about ...

All About Your Performance

I started ...

Ending

Reflect

Did I begin with a question to the audience?

Yes / No

E Practice with a friend. Then share with your class.

Write About It

A Read the diary entry. Underline the time phrases and circle the commas.

Dear Diary,

What an amazing night! Before the talent show, my friend Malik was really scared and nervous. He was still practicing his dance at 7:15, and I was helping him backstage. Then, he went on stage at 7:30! His sister and his parents were sitting near the stage, but Malik wasn't looking at them at all. He was just dancing and doing his best. The audience was clapping and shouting the whole time! After the show, everyone was taking pictures of Malik. He was tired but happy. My friend's a star!

Look
When the time phrase is at the beginning, we use a comma.

B Move the time phrase and rewrite the sentences.

1 My sister was singing at 8:00 last night.
At 8:00 last night, my sister was singing.

2 Before the performance, she was feeling nervous.

3 We were waiting for her after the show.

4 Her teacher was making a video during the show.

5 At 8:30, the singers were walking off the stage.

C Plan. Think about a time you watched a performance. Complete.

What was happening?	What were you doing?	What were the performers doing?	What was the audience doing?

Reflect
Did I use time phrases? Did I use commas in the right places?

D Write about the performance in your diary.

Read the questions and draw or write your answers.

What did I do?

What did I learn?

What was my favorite part?

How well did I do?

What can I do next?

I'm Jake. What animal do I want to take pictures of? Find out in Unit 5.

UNIT 3
UNIT 4

Come to the Show!

START

You're very hungry. Go to the pizza shop.

How much money is this?

Stop! Buy a hat and count your change. Miss a turn.

The crew needs you backstage. Miss a turn.

Do you have to help your parents at home? What do you do?

You sell your hat for $2.00. Go ahead two spaces.

What were you doing at noon yesterday?

12:00 PM

An actor is away. Your have to learn the script. Miss a turn.

Do you have to clean your room?

Did you spend any money yesterday? What did you buy?

You need a costume. Go back to the hat shop.

You forgot to buy a gift for friend. Go back to the hat shop.

Imagine you had the day off from school. What could you do?

What was your teacher doing five minutes ago?

Do you have a cheap ticket or an expensive ticket?

SCHOOL PLAY Front Row $2

HOW TO PLAY

1. Play with a partner. Make counters.
2. Flip a coin to move one or two spaces.
3. When you land on a square, follow the directions or answer the question.
4. The first player to get to the show is the winner.

What were you doing at 8:30 this morning?

Are you usually late, early, or on time?

Go to the café. Your friend is waiting for you there.

Eat your pizza. Miss a turn.

What were you and your friends doing before this class?

Stop! Buy a drink. Miss a turn.

Were you watching TV at 8 o'clock last night?

You found $5.00. What should you do?

You have to paint the set on stage. Miss a turn.

What do these mean? + − =

You found these coins. Should you spend them?

You lost your wallet. Go back to the café.

Was your family eating dinner at 6:30 last night?

What do you save your money for?

Go to a rehearsal. Miss a turn.

What does the customer have to buy?

The actor is back! You don't have to perform. Go ahead two spaces.

Stop! You didn't pay for your ticket. Miss a turn.

Stop! You're feeling very nervous. Miss a turn.

What was happening at 7:00 last night?

FINISH

The actors are ready! Go ahead one space.

UNIT 5

Make Some Noise

A Listen and find. Is this place quiet or noisy?

B Listen, say, and number the pictures in **A**.

C Close your eyes. Listen, visualize, and say.

D Look and write.

1 Whistle a song.
2 Bees ______ .
3 Birds ______ .
4 ______ a secret.
5 Frogs ______ .
6 Cookies ______ .
7 The chairs ______ .
8 Dogs ______ .

E Listen and complete. Then watch and sing.

Are You Awake?

Are you awake?
I hear a **1** crunch . *What is it?*
I hear a **2** *w* ______ . *What's that sound?*

I'm awake at midnight
I'm listening carefully
I hear scary noises all around me
There's a **3** s ______ on the stairs
What's happening?
I'm scared! My eyes are big and round.

"Are you awake?"
I **4** w ______ in my sister's ear.
There's a **5** b ______ on the door
I'm hugging my pillow
I'm listening carefully
I'm quiet and I don't make any noise
There's a really loud **6** c ______
and the light comes on!
"Oh! Mom! Sorry, you fell on our toys!"

Explore Language

A Listen and read. What's Jake's plan?

Grandma:	Jake! What are you doing?
Jake:	I'm going to look for birds in the forest. Birds wake up early.
Grandma:	Are you going to come back for breakfast?
Jake:	No, I'm going to stay there all morning. Can I take my breakfast with me?
Grandma:	Sure. So, what are you going to do in the forest all morning?
Jake:	I'm going to sit quietly and look for owls. I'm not going to make any noise. Then, I'm going to take pictures.
Grandma:	But most owls are awake only at night.
Jake:	Oh! Then, I'm going to go back to bed!

B Look at **A**. Complete.

***Going to* Statements**

I	___	___	look for	birds.
		not ___	make	any noise.

We aren't = We're not
She isn't = She's not
but only use I'm not

Remember

C Think and discuss. Then choose.

1 We use *going to* to talk about a plan / a decision in the future.

D Listen and say.

E Read and complete.

1 She's going to visit (visit) her grandparents this weekend.

2 I ___ (not bang) on the door at Grandma's house!

3 We ___ (play) with our dog after school.

4 Listen! I ___ (whisper) my phone number in your ear.

5 My teacher ___ (not be) at school tomorrow because she's sick.

6 The restaurants ___ (not open) before noon.

F Play a game. Think about what you're going to do after school today. Mime and guess.

Why are there different kinds of music?

A Listen. What does Rashid learn about the cello?

drums ☐

violin ☐

cello ☐

trumpet ☐

conductor 1

orchestra ☐

flute ☐

piano ☐

harp ☐

xylophone ☐

clarinet ☐

B Listen, say, and number the pictures in **A**.

C Read and choose.

1 My mother plays the cello / conductor in an trumpet / orchestra.

2 The conductor / piano tells the musicians to play quickly!

3 My father plays the violin / clarinet and the flute / xylophone. He has to blow into them to make a sound.

4 My baby brother likes to bang pots and pans. I'm going to get him some real harps / drums soon.

5 The harp / orchestra is made from wood, but it looks like gold!

D Now listen to Derick and María. What do they think about their music classes?

Derick, USA

María, Venezuela

E Listen again. Complete.

🇺🇸	🇬🇧
program	programme

1 María plays the violin every day and on weekends.

2 Derick plays the ______________ at school.

3 María's going to join a famous ______________ some day.

4 Derick's going to ______________ drums some day.

5 Both Derick and María love their ______________ programs.

Is music important to you? Why?
Where can people hear music in your community?

Explore Language

A Listen and read. What are Jen and Carla planning?

1

2

3

Mom: What are you going to make?

Jen: Drums and a guitar. Then, we're going to have a show!

Mom: Really! Where is it going to be?

Jen: Here. I'm going to move these chairs.

Carla: I'm going to make tickets.

Mom: When is the show going to be?

Jen: Tomorrow!

Mom: Are you going to practice the music now?

Jen: No, we aren't. We have to make everything first.

Mom: I see. Who's going to buy the tickets?

Jen: Oh. We didn't think about that.

Carla: Maybe our moms?

Mom: Good idea!

US	UK
have a show	do a show

B Look at A. Complete.

***Going to* Questions**

What	____		you	going	to	make?
When	____		the show	____		be?
Who	____	going	____	____	the tickets?	Our moms.
____	you		____	practice the music now?	Yes, we are.	No, we ____.

We say *What're*, but we write *What are*.

Remember

C Think and discuss. Then choose.

1 We use *going to* in questions to ask about plans in the future / past.

D Listen and say.

E Read and complete.

1 What's he going to play?
He's going to play the clarinet.

2 ______________ the harp?
Yes, she is.

3 ______________ the piano?
No, they aren't.

4 Who ______________ the cello?
No one.

5 ______________ the drums?
No, he isn't.

F Play *I'm a Detective!* Each person writes sentences. Put them all in a pile. Then find out who's going to do it.

I'm going to ride my bike tonight.

Do you have a bike?

Yes, I do.

Are you going to ride your bike tonight?

Yes, I am. It's me!

Talk About It

A Watch and listen. Do Otis and Lewis agree in the end?

B Watch again. Check (✔) the phrases you hear.

1. ✔ I love music. It's my favorite.
2. ◯ But I think music is more important.
3. ◯ I disagree.
4. ◯ In my opinion, music is the most important class.
5. ◯ That's not true.
6. ◯ I didn't think about that.
7. ◯ That's a good point.
8. ◯ You're right. Music is important!

Pronunciation /θ/ and /tʃ/

Listen and say.

math | with | both | much | watch | each

What other words do you know with these sounds?

C Plan. Which class do you think is the most important? Complete.

I think ______________________ class is the most important because …

1 ______________________

2 ______________________

3 ______________________

D Prepare your conversation. Use your ideas from **C** and phrases from **B**.

A

Give your opinion

In my opinion, … ______________________

Agree or disagree

____

Give a reason

____

B

Give your opinion

____

Ask for a reason

____

Show understanding

____

Reflect
Did I respond to my friend's ideas politely?
Yes / No

E Practice with a friend.

Write About It

A Read the paragraph. Underline the words people said and circle the sound words.

The Sounds Around Us

My City Soundscape

I'm going to tell you about the sounds from my apartment window on a hot, summer afternoon. I heard lots of cars go by. I heard tires squeak. Then a man shouted, "Watch where you're going!" Three dogs were barking loudly. A woman called, "Stop barking!" but the dogs didn't stop. Lots of children were shouting and laughing. One little kid said, "Wait for me!" I heard music in my friend's apartment, and a baby cried, "Mama! Mama!" Someone's door shut with a bang. Then my mom called, "Come and help with dinner", so I left my window.

apartment | flat

B Rewrite. Add a comma and quotation marks.

1 The police officer shouted Look out!

The police officer shouted, "Look out!"

2 His mother called Time for dinner!

3 My little sister asked Can you help me?

4 The boy said Hurry up!

5 My dad said Please clean your room.

C Plan. Think about your soundscape. Close your eyes and imagine. Complete.

Where were you?

Who did you hear?

What did you hear?

What did they say?

Reflect
Did I use quotation marks around what people said?

D Write about your soundscape.

Read the questions and draw or write your answers.

How well did I do?

What can I do next?

Hello! I'm Carla. What's my favorite food? Find out in Unit 6.

UNIT 6 That Looks Good

A Listen and find. What happened to the strawberries?

🇺🇸	🇬🇧
trash can	rubbish bin

B Listen, say, and number the pictures in **A**.

C Close your eyes. Listen, visualize, and say.

D Look and write.

What do I use?	What do I do?
trash can	

The *best* food is ______________ food!

E Listen and complete. Then watch and sing.

That Looks Good!

Look in the 1 fridge (gefrid). What do you see?
I see fruit and vegetables calling to me!
All the fruit and vegetables, cold and 2 ______________ (hfser)
3 ______________ (tcu pu) into pieces—they're the best!
Look on the 4 ______________ (vetso). What do you see?
You're cooking something special, just for me!
5 ______________ (yfr) some eggs and potatoes, delicious and hot,
6 ______________ (xmi) it with cheese—I like it a lot!
Look on the 7 ______________ (lglir). What do you see?
A piece of meat and vegetables there for me!
Ping goes the 8 ______________ (wmaevirco). My food is done.
Choosing what I want to eat is so much fun!

Explore Language

A Listen and read. Who's going to wash the dishes?

B Look at **A**. Complete.

Infinitives

I	plan	to	________	fruit salad for my family.
	don't ________		________	meat.
Alec	________	____	wash	dishes!

Would you	________	to	________	more potatoes?

I like to play, not ~~*I like play*~~.
I like to play, not ~~*I enjoy to play*~~.

Watch Out

C Think and discuss. Then choose.

1 When we use the infinitive, *to* comes before / after the second verb.

2 We use *would like* to be more / less polite.

D Listen and say.

E Read and complete.

I 1 love to eat (love, eat) fruit! My sister and I 2 ________ (try, eat) fruit every day. First, we 3 ________ (need, wash) the fruit. We 4 ________ (not need, wash) mangos or bananas because she always peels them. Sometimes, she 5 ________ (like, peel) apples and peaches, too. Then, I always 6 ________ (choose, cut up) the fruit. I 7 ________ (like, mix) the pieces together into a fresh fruit salad.

F Choose and write sentences with infinitives. How many can you make? Compare.

like start want try
plan hate need love

eat grill drink fry
make cook peel mix

I like to eat watermelon every day.

My dad doesn't want to grill chicken for dinner.

How do people stay healthy?

A Listen to the food scientist. Which foods have protein?

B Listen, say, and number the pictures in **A**.

C Read and choose the correct answer.

1 Your body gets carbohydrates / protein from meat, fish, and eggs.
2 You should eat fruit and vegetables once a week / every day.
3 Bread and pasta are made from grains / meat.
4 Dairy / Sugar helps to make your bones strong.
5 You should have a little bit of / no fat every day.
6 Cookies / Strawberries are something sweet and healthy.

D Now listen to Min-jun and Francesca. How are their lunches the same?

Min-jun, South Korea

Francesca, Italy

E Listen again. Check (✔) what they eat.

Who eats …	Min-jun	Francesca
1 soup?	✔	○
2 rice?	○	○
3 vegetables?	○	○
4 meat or fish?	○	○
5 pasta?	○	○
6 fruit?	○	○

What's your favorite meal?
What can people do to eat healthier meals?

Explore Language

A Listen and read. Why doesn't Tim cry?

B Look at **A**. Complete.

Gerunds

I	________	making	new dishes.
Alec	________	________	onions.
Tim	________		
Do you	like	________	?

I like playing. =
I like to play.
I enjoy playing, not
~~*I enjoy to play.*~~

Remember

C Think and discuss. Then choose.

1 We use *–ing* / *–ed* at the end of a verb to make a gerund.

2 We use *–ing* to use a verb as a noun / adjective.

D Listen and say.

E Read and complete.

1 Evan enjoys eating (eat) sandwiches for lunch.

2 Ana keeps ________ (put) butter on her potatoes.

3 My mother doesn't like ________ (cook) dinner every day.

4 My classmates don't mind ________ (wait) for our lunch.

5 We love ________ (eat) fruit and vegetables every day.

6 My dad doesn't mind ________ (shop) for food.

F Play *Who Is It?* Write about three friends. Then read and guess in groups of three.

She loves singing. She hates cleaning her desk.

She likes asking questions. Who is she?

Talk About It

A Watch and listen. What does Stephen choose for his salad?

Watch
How does the server make her guest feel comfortable?

B Watch again. Check (✔) the phrases you hear.

1. ✔ Welcome to The Friendly Tomato!
2. ◯ I'm going to be your server.
3. ◯ Would you like something to drin k?
4. ◯ First, choose your main green vegetable.
5. ◯ I want to try black beans!
6. ◯ I'd like some fruit, please.
7. ◯ What about carbohydrates?

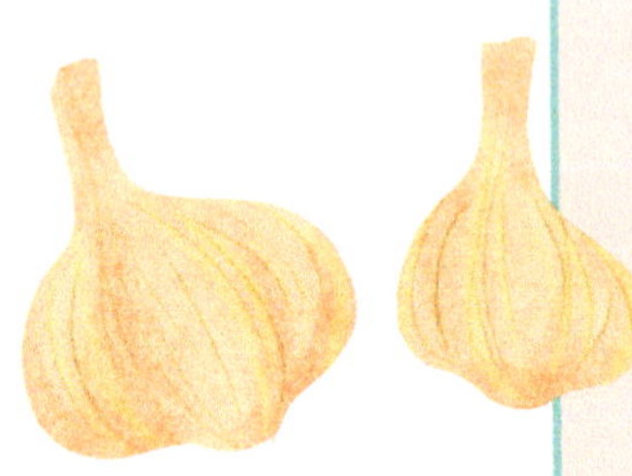

🇺🇸	🇬🇧
server	waiter/waitress

Pronunciation /fr/ and /bl/

Listen and say.

friendly fruit from blog black blue

What other words do you know with these sounds?

C Plan. Think about your restaurant. Complete.

Restaurant name

Menu

Food on my menu

- **Protein**
- **Dairy**
- **Carbohydrates**
- **Fruit**
- **Fat**
- **Vegetables**

D Prepare your conversation. Use your ideas from **C** and phrases from **B**.

A

Greet your customer

Welcome to …

Ask a question

Ask another question

B

Say thank you

Give an answer

Respond and say thank you

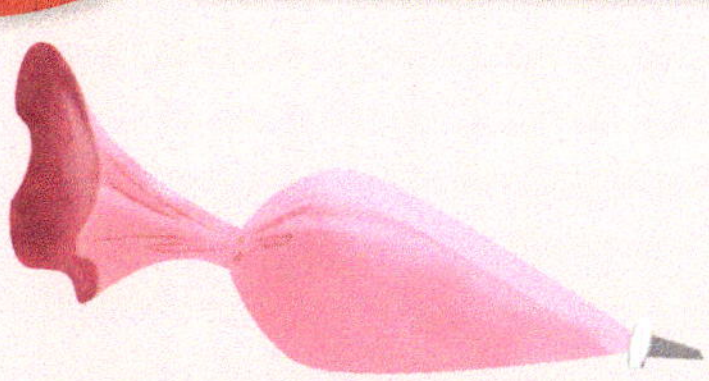

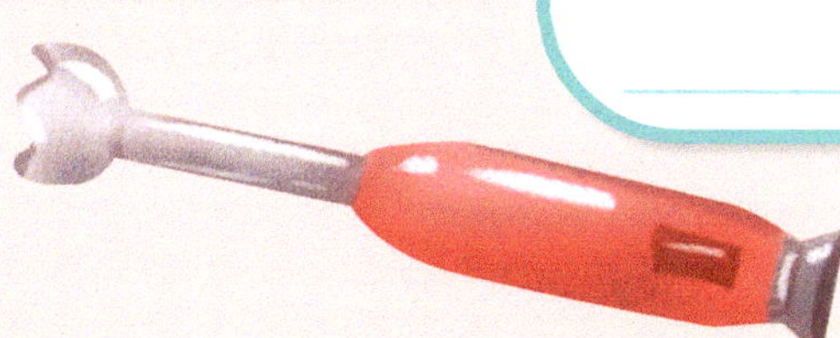

E Practice with a friend.

Reflect
Did I make my guest comfortable?
Yes / No

Write About It

A Read the report. Circle the four headings.

My Food Experiment

Question

Am I a healthy eater?

Method

I kept a food diary for one day. I wrote down everything I ate. Then I counted everything up. Here is what I ate.

Results

Breakfast: cereal, milk, orange juice, grapes

Lunch: egg sandwich on white bread, apple, cookies, water

Dinner: rice, chicken, tomato sauce, cheese, bread, olive oil, milk, water

Fruit: 3
Vegetables: 0
Protein: 2
Carbohydrates: 4
Dairy: 3
Fat: 1
Water: 2
Sweets: 1

Conclusions

1 I eat a lot of carbohydrates.
2 I need to drink more water.
3 I should eat more vegetables.

B Match each heading to the correct sentence.

1 Question
2 Method
3 Results
4 Conclusion

a. Carbohydrates: 6
b. I learned I should drink more water.
c. I kept a food diary for one day
d. Am I a healthy eater?

C Plan. Keep a food diary for one day. Use the method in **A**. Then write down your results. What are your conclusions?

Breakfast: ____
Lunch: ____
Dinner: ____

Fruit: ____ Dairy: ____ Water: ____
Vegetables: ____ Carbohydrates: ____ Sweets: ____
Protein: ____ Fat: ____
My Conclusion: ____

Reflect
Did I write something for each heading?

D Write about your experiment.

Read the questions and draw or write your answers.

What did I do?

What did I learn?

What was my favorite part?

How well did I do?

What can I do next?

Hello! I'm Alec. How am I helping my dad? Find out in Unit 7.

UNIT 5

UNIT 6

Say Three

Your plans for the future.

I want to …

I plan to …

I'm going to …

Move 3 spaces

What your family likes to make for dinner.

We like …

Sometimes we …

And we always …

Three different instruments in an orchestra.

There's …

And there's …

And there are …

_________'s Points

_________'s Points

Add 3 points

GO Start

Add 3 extra points

Talk about your kitchen at home.

My kitchen …

There's …

There aren't …

Say what you're going to do this weekend.

I'm …

And I'm …

But I'm not …

Things!

Say what you hate doing.

I hate …

And I don't like …

And I really hate …

What sounds can you hear right now?

There's a …

Someone's …

A/The (bird)'s …

Move 3 spaces

_______'s Points

_______'s Points

HOW TO PLAY

1 Play in pairs or small groups.

2 Use your spinner to move around the board.

3 When you land on a square, say three things.

4 Color a square in your Points Chart for every sentence you say.

5 The first player to get 20 points is the winner.

What is your friend going to do after school?

He/She's …

And he/she's …

But he/she isn't …

Describe a healthy dinner.

There's …

There are …

There aren't …

Move 3 spaces

What does your family enjoy doing on the weekends?

We enjoy …

We like to …

But we don't …

Talk about musical instruments.

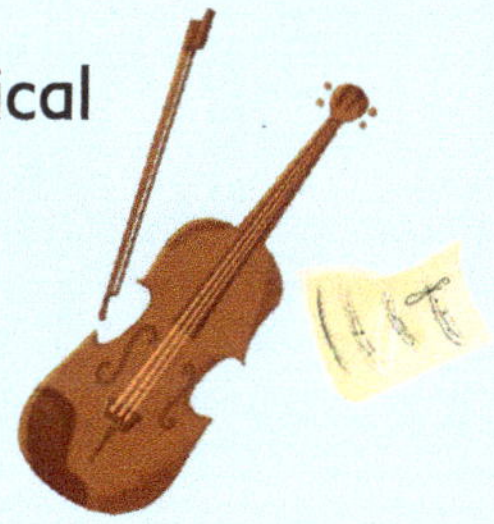

I like the …

I can play …

I love the …

UNIT 7

How Can We Help?

A Listen and find. Where's the family going?

B Listen, say, and number the pictures in **A**.

C Close your eyes. Listen, visualize, and say.

D Look and write.

Emergency

Adjectives:	Person:	Place:	Transportation:
______	______	______	______
______			______

E Listen and complete. Then watch and sing.

fire truck | fire engine

Emergency Helpers

They're coming! They're coming! They're answering our call!
They're coming here to help us in no time at all!

Police officers tell the drivers what to do,
They keep us **1** safe at home, at school, and in bad weather, too!
The drivers of the **2** a__________ go very, very fast,
They care for us and get us to the hospital at last!

Firefighters put out fires day and night,
On a fire truck or a **3** h__________, they hold on tight!
4 R__________ w__________ come to help in an **5** e__________,
They take us to a **6** s__________, a clean, warm place to be.

Explore Language

A Listen and read. What's Hassan doing?

Dad: Everyone from Main Street is here!

Alec: There's the woman who works in the café down the street.

Dad: And that man drives a truck.

Alec: The people who drive the ambulance are here, too. I think everyone's safe.

Dad: I'm glad about that. Do you see Hassan?

Alec: Who's he?

Dad: He's the rescue worker who came to our store.

Alec: Look, he's telling a story to those kids. He's flying a helicopter!

Dad: Let's go and thank him again. He did a great job!

truck
lorry

B Look at **A**. Complete.

Relative Clauses: *Who*

There	's	the woman	who	works	in the café down the street.
He	______	the rescue worker	______	______	to our store.
The people		______	______	the ambulance are here.	

Watch Out

That's the man who ~~he~~ flies the helicopter.

C **Think and discuss. Then choose.**

1 We use clauses beginning with *who* to give more information about places / people.

D **Listen and say.**

E **Underline the relative clause in each sentence.**

1 There's the boy who wants to be a firefighter.

2 Martin's the police officer who directs traffic.

3 The people who drive the ambulance are very kind.

4 The woman who helps at the shelter is my mom.

5 Maria's the girl who wants to fly a helicopter.

6 The rescue workers are the people who keep us safe.

F **Look around your classroom. Complete and compare. Do you agree?**

1 The student who wears the coolest glasses is ______________________ .

2 The student who's the funniest is ______________________ .

3 The student who can sing the best is ______________________ .

4 The student who jumps the highest is ______________________ .

5 The student who ______________________________ is me!

student

pupil

The student who's the funniest is ...

Jason!

Yes! I agree. Jason's the funniest!

How can we prepare before an emergency?

A Listen to Jonas talking about natural disasters. Why does he want to be a storm chaser?

B Listen, say, and number the pictures in **A**.

C Read and match.

1 lots of snow falling down a mountain — a. tsunami
2 many trees burning over a large area — b. avalanche
3 a huge wave from the ocean — c. volcano
4 a dangerous storm with very strong wind — d. forest fire
5 when the ground and all the buildings shake — e. earthquake
6 a mountain which pushes hot lava and ash out — f. hurricane

D Now listen to Mely and Dustin. What do they practice at school?

Mely, Philippines

Dustin, USA

E Listen again. Write *True* or *False*.

1 An earthquake under the ocean can cause a huge wave. True
2 Mely goes to a shelter after an earthquake. ______
3 You should cover your head in an earthquake. ______
4 A tornado comes very slowly. ______
5 Dustin hides in a shelter during a tornado. ______
6 Earthquakes and tornadoes are dangerous. ______

How can you and your family be ready for an emergency? What is your school's emergency plan?

Explore Language

A Listen and read. What do Hassan and Alec find?

 Grammar Relative Clauses: *That*

B Look at A. Complete.

Relative Clauses: *That*

This	is	the wall	that	stopped	the flood.
Those	are	things	______	______	here.
There	's	a backpack	______	______	someone's homework inside.
People			______	______	things can find them.

Look

That is a relative pronoun. It comes at the beginning of a relative clause.

C Think and discuss. Then choose.

1 We use clauses beginning with *that* to give more information about things / people / things or people.

D Listen and say.

E Make new sentences with *that*.

1 This is the helicopter. The helicopter stopped the forest fire.

This is the helicopter that stopped the forest fire.

2 I heard the avalanche. The avalanche covered our village with snow.

____

3 They remember the earthquake. The earthquake shook their house.

____

4 We escaped the tsunami. The tsunami came after the earthquake.

____

5 Hassan found a backpack. The backpack had Zack's homework in it.

____

F Play *Silly Sentences*. Complete and say. Who has the silliest sentences?

I live in a house that …
I go to a school that …
I have a friend that …
I want a backpack that …
I have a toy that …

I live in a house that has 500 rooms!

I go to a school that is made from cookies!

Take the Stage

A Watch and listen. Why does Otis want to be a rescue worker?

Watch
How does he show that he is excited about his topic?

B Watch again. Check (✔) the phrases you hear.

1. ✔ I'd like to be a rescue worker when I grow up.
2. ◯ Here are my reasons why.
3. ◯ First, rescue workers travel all over the world.
4. ◯ Next, rescue workers know a lot about the body.
5. ◯ Finally, rescue workers are friendly and helpful.
6. ◯ They help people feel safe in emergencies.
7. ◯ That's why I'd like to be one, too.

Pronunciation /str/ and /tr/

Listen and say.

straight stressed strong travel truck try

What other words do you know with these sounds?

C Plan. Think about important helpers. Would you like to be one? Complete.

I would like / wouldn't like to be a ______________________________ .

Reasons why or why not

______	______	______
______	______	______

D Prepare your presentation. Use your ideas from **C** and phrases from **B**.

Introduction

When I grow up ...

Reasons

Here are my reasons why.

Ending

Reflect
Did I sound excited about my topic?
Yes / No

E Practice with a friend. Then share with your class.

Write About It

A Read the story. Circle the quotation marks and underline the exclamation points.

Tornado!

"Look!" called Mom. Dad and I looked up. We saw a long, dark cloud that was spinning around. The wind was very strong.

"It's a tornado!" shouted Dad. "Quick! Into the shelter!"

We ran behind the house. Dad opened a small door in the ground. Inside were stairs, but it was very dark.

"You go first!" yelled Dad. I didn't want to go, but Mom took my hand.

"I'm here, John," she said.

Suddenly, I remembered my cat Frosty.

"Dad!" I shouted. "Frosty's in the house!"

"Let me get him," said Dad. "Stay with Mom."

Mom and I went down the stairs. Mom pulled the door shut and lit a candle. It was quiet. Together we sat and waited.

exclamation point (US)	exclamation mark (UK)

B Read what John and his mom said later. Add the correct punctuation. Use (!) or (.). Then add quotation marks (" ").

1 Be careful called Mom "Be careful!" called Mom.

2 I need to find Frosty I shouted ______

3 Please help us we called to the rescue worker ______

4 We're down here Mom and I shouted ______

5 You're safe now I whispered to my cat ______

C Plan. How does the story end? Write.

What happens to Dad?	What happens to Frosty?	Who comes to help?
______	______	______
What does Dad say?	**What do you say to Frosty?**	**What does the helper say?**
______	______	______

Reflect
Did I use exclamation points to show excitement?

D Write your own ending to the story. Use your ideas from **C**.

Read the questions and draw or write your answers.

What did I do? What did I learn? How did I learn?

How well did I do?

Hello! I'm Hassan. Where do I go on vacation? Find out in Unit 8.

What can I do next?

UNIT 8

Under the Sea

A Listen and find. Why do the fish swim away?

B Listen, say, and number the pictures in A.

C Close your eyes. Listen, visualize, and say.

D Look and write.

Fish	Not fish	
seahorse	octopus	

E Listen and complete. Then watch and sing.

Under the Sea

What do you see under the sea?
Look down through the glass and describe it to me!
We take care of living things under the sea
So they can keep growing, alive and free!

I see a 1 whale  as big as a truck,

And 2 ______________  having fun,

I see some 3 ______________  floating nearby,
Yellow and pink like the sun!

I see a 4 ______________  swimming along,

And a 5 ______________  down on the sand.

I see a 6 ______________,  orange and white,
Keep going! I'm not ready to go back to land.

ocean floor
seabed

Explore Language

A Listen and read. What's the word for a group of fish that swims together?

1

Ahmad: Is that a coral reef?

Guide: Yes, it is. Lots of different kinds of coral grow here.

2

Guide: The reef is a shelter for small fish. They often swim into the coral and hide from sharks and other large fish.

3

Ahmad: Look at those angelfish! They're swimming through the coral right now!

4

Ahmad: Why are the fish swimming together like that?

Guide: It helps them stay safe. It's called a school of fish.

5

Ahmad: That's a school? Cool! I like their uniforms.

B Look at **A**. Complete.

Simple Present

They often	______	into the coral and hide.
______	that a coral reef?	

Present Progressive

They	're	______	through the coral right now!
Why	______	the fish ______	together like that?

often, *always*, or *usually* = simple present
now = present progressive

Look

C Think and discuss. Then choose.

1 We use the simple present / present progressive to talk about something that happens often or every day.

2 We use the simple present / present progressive to talk about something that is happening now.

D Listen and say.

E Read and complete.

1 The small fish usually go over the coral, but today they're going under it. (go)

2 The shark often ______ down to the ocean floor, but now it ______ up to the boats. (swim)

3 Every day, those clownfish ______ on the ocean floor, but right now they ______ in the coral. (hide)

4 Today we ______ around the pool, but usually we ______ across it. (swim)

F Play *Under The Sea*. You're a fish. Mime an activity you do often. Guess and ask.

You're looking for food!

Yes!

How often do you look for food?

I look for food every day!

Why is sea life important?

A Listen to Anya and Dean talk about fish. Why are they different shapes and colors?

- striped 1
- spotted ☐
- round ☐
- flat ☐
- clear ☐
- aquarium ☐
- horizontal ☐
- vertical ☐
- protect ☐
- save ☐

B Listen, say, and number the pictures in **A**.

C Read and complete. Then match.

1 A jellyfish is clear, so — a. go up and down.
2 An angelfish is f__________, so — b. big fish can't see it.
3 A clownfish is s__________, so — c. it can hide in small places.
4 V__________ stripes — d. it can hide behind coral.
5 An a__________ is a place that — e. protects fish.

D Now listen to Yasmin and Li Li. What's special about their aquariums?

Yasmin, United Arab Emirates

Li Li, China

E Listen again. Check (✔) the correct city.

Which aquarium …	Dubai	Shanghai
1 has a very long tunnel?	○	✔
2 teaches people about sharks?	○	○
3 has fish from China?	○	○
4 has a very large window?	○	○
5 is in the United Arab Emirates?	○	○
6 is one of the largest in the world?	○	○

What can you do to help protect the sea?
Where can people learn more about the sea?

Explore Language

A Listen and read. What are the boys going to do?

1

2

Ahmad: There are dangerous fish here.

Daniel: Lionfish? How are they dangerous?

Ahmad: People brought them from far away. Now, they live here and eat everything!

Daniel: What will happen to the fish that live here? Will they have food?

Ahmad: No, they won't. The lionfish will eat it all!

Daniel: Hey, this poster says we can help!

Ahmad: How?

Daniel: We'll catch some lionfish! Then, there won't be so many.

Ahmad: But that sign says "No Fishing".

Daniel: This is different! We won't catch any other fish—only lionfish!

B Look at **A**. Complete.

Future: Predictions with *Will*

We	'll	catch	some lionfish.
We	______		any other fish.

What	______	happen	to the fish that live here?

______	they	______	food?	Yes, they ______ .	No, they ______ .

will not = won't
they will = they'll
Look

C Think and discuss. Then choose.

1 We use *will* + infinitive to make predictions about the future / the past.

D Listen and say.

E Put the words in order.

1 will / clean again. / the seawater / be / In three years,
In three years, the seawater will be clean again.

2 won't / You / many fish / catch / tomorrow.

______

3 the aquarium / again / next year? / visit / you / Will

______

4 in the future. / save / will / the coral reefs / about sea life / People who care

______

5 the sand / Next week, / warmer / will / at the beach. / be

______

6 my family / Next summer, / go / will / on vacation.

______

F Play a game. Predict the future. What will sea life be like in ten years?

There won't be any lionfish here.

We'll have boats that don't use gasoline.

A Watch and listen. What happened after people stopped catching blue whales?

Watch
How does she interest the audience at the beginning of her presentation?

B Watch again. Check (✔) the phrases you hear.

1. ✔ My presentation today is about blue whales.
2. ◯ It's as heavy as two horses.
3. ◯ A long time ago, there were lots of blue whales.
4. ◯ But then people with fast boats were worried.
5. ◯ Soon there were almost no blue whales left.
6. ◯ As a result, people stopped catching whales.
7. ◯ Today, we protect whales.

Pronunciation /h/ and /w/

Listen and say.

heavy huge hard whale were worried

What other words do you know with these sounds?

C Plan. Think about a sea creature you learned about in this unit. How can we protect it? Check (✔) and complete.

Problem	Solution
	◯ don't throw trash on the ground or in the sea
	◯ stop hunting them
	◯ put some of them in zoos or aquariums
Description	

D Prepare your presentation. Use your ideas from **C** and phrases from **B**.

Introduction

My presentation today is about ...

Middle

The problem ...

Ending

As a result ...

Reflect
Did I say something interesting at the beginning of my presentation?
Yes / No

E Practice with a friend. Then share with your class.

Write About It

A Read the concrete poems. Why do they look like this?

Fish

little fish
quick and colorful
swimming in the sea, turning
fast, hiding in the coral, purple and
blue and orange and yellow
Are you in your
school?

Starfish

like
a star
in the sky
you lie down in the soft ocean sand
with all five arms
You're a tiny star
of the sea and I think
you're very beautiful
but not shiny!

B Look at **A**. Find synonyms for these words and phrases. Write.

1 quick fast
2 very small ______
3 sea ______
4 pretty ______
5 purple, blue, orange, and yellow ______

C Plan. Think about a topic for your concrete poem. Complete.

Topic	Words to use	
______	______	______
Shape	______	______
______	______	______

D Write your concrete poem.

1 Write your topic as the title.
2 Draw the shape you want to use.
3 Write your words inside the shape. They don't have to rhyme!
4 Use a word and its synonym somewhere in your poem.
5 End your poem with a question mark or an exclamation point!

Reflect
Did I use a synonym and did I spell it correctly?

Read the questions and draw or write your answers.

What did I do?

What did I learn?

What was my favorite part?

How well did I do?

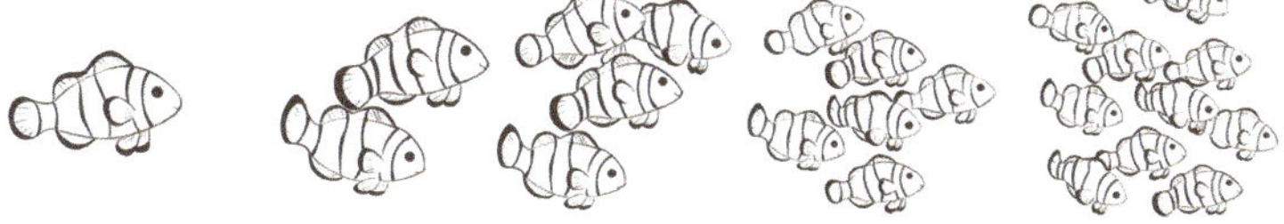

Hello! I'm Daniel. How do I feel? Find out in Unit 9.

What can I do next?

UNIT 7

UNIT 8

Crossword Clues

Student A

Across

6

10

9

12

Down

3

4

What's 9 across?

It's something that ...

Student B

Across **Down**

1

2

7

What's 7 down?

11

5

8
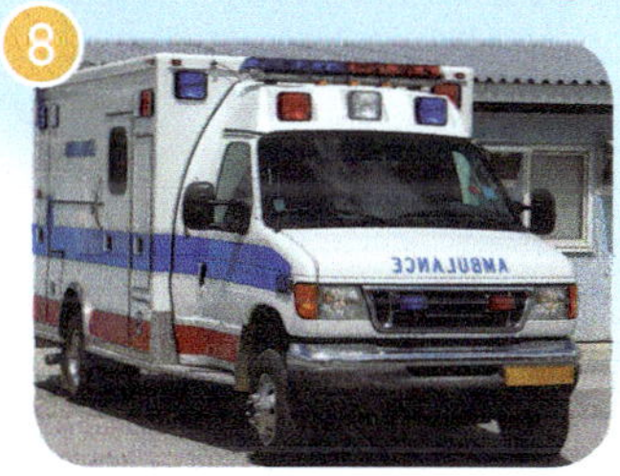

It's an animal that ...

HOW TO PLAY

1 Look at the pictures and write the words in your crossword.

2 Next, take turns asking about the missing clues.

3 Explain each clue without saying the word. Your partner has to guess and write.

4 Then, you ask, guess, and write.

5 When you finish, compare your crosswords. Who wrote more words?

UNIT 9 What's the Matter?

A Listen and find. What's the matter with number three?

🇺🇸	🇬🇧
have a fever, sick	have a temperature, ill

B Listen, say, and number the pictures in A.

C Close your eyes. Listen, visualize, and say.

D Look and write. Some words are used twice.

I have …
a stomachache

I'm going to …

I'm/I feel …

E Listen and complete. Then watch and sing.

What's the Matter?

What's the matter? Are you OK?
I don't feel well. I'm sick today.

What's the matter? You don't look well.
I have a bad **1** c__________ ,
I'm **2** c__________ and **3** s__________ ,
I have a **4** h__________ .
I need a break!

What's the matter? You look sad.
I feel really **5** d__________ and have a
6 s__________ .
I ate a lot in town, and I need to
lie down!
What's the matter? Do you feel bad?
Yes, I have a **7** f__________ ,
I don't know what to do,
Because I also have an **8** e__________
and a sore throat, too!

Explore Language

A Listen and read. What happened to the sign and the skeleton?

Daniel:	George, are you OK?
George:	I feel dizzy. What happened?
Daniel:	I was standing over there when I heard a loud noise!
George:	I heard it, too! I was standing next to those balloons when they popped.
Daniel:	What were you doing when that sign fell down?
George:	I was listening to the doctor when it fell down. It hit me and I fell down, too!
Daniel:	Were you holding the skeleton when the sign hit you?
George:	No, I wasn't.
Daniel:	You weren't holding it when you fell, but you're holding it now!
George:	Ha ha!

B Look at **A**. Complete.

Past Progressive with *When*

What	______	you ______		when	that sign	______	down?
I	______	listening	to the doctor	______	it	______	down.
You	______	______	the skeleton	______	you	______ .	
Were	you	______	the skeleton	______	the sign	______	you?
Yes, I ______ .				No, I ______ .			

Remember

Past progressive negative = *wasn't/weren't* + *–ing*
Simple past negative = *didn't*

C Think and discuss. Then choose.

1 We use the simple past / past progressive to talk about a continuing action in the past.

2 To show that an action interrupted another action, we use *who* / *when*.

D Listen and say.

E Read and complete. Write about you.

1 It was raining when I woke up this morning.

2 I ______________________ when mom called me for dinner.

3 We ______________________ when the teacher came into the classroom.

4 My friends and I were having fun when ______________________ .

5 My friend was walking to school when ______________________ .

6 My family was eating dinner when ______________________ .

F Play *Silly Conversation*. Complete and say. Who has the silliest sentences?

What were you doing when ...
the cheetah ran by?
the dolphins jumped?
the lightning started?
the helicopter landed?

What were you doing when the cheetah ran by?

I was baking cookies when the cheetah ran by.

Why are doctors and nurses important?

A Listen to a nurse who works at a community clinic. When do people go to the hospital?

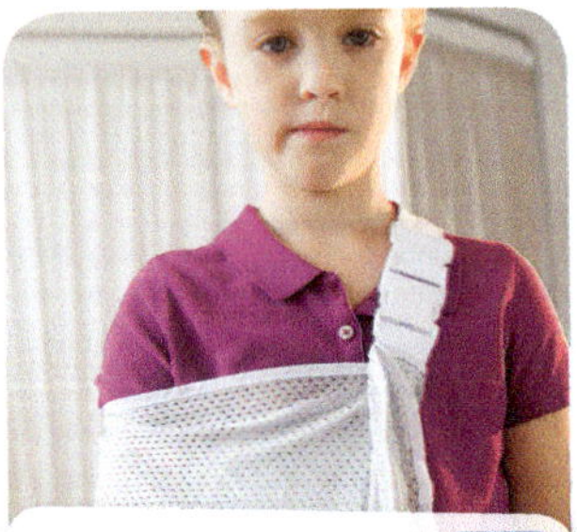

broken arm ☐

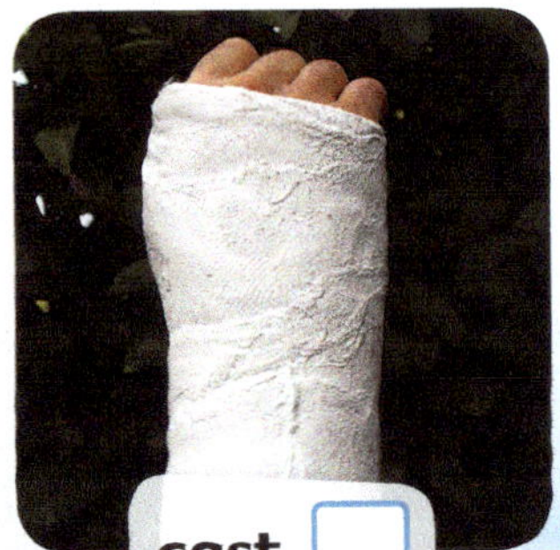

cast ☐

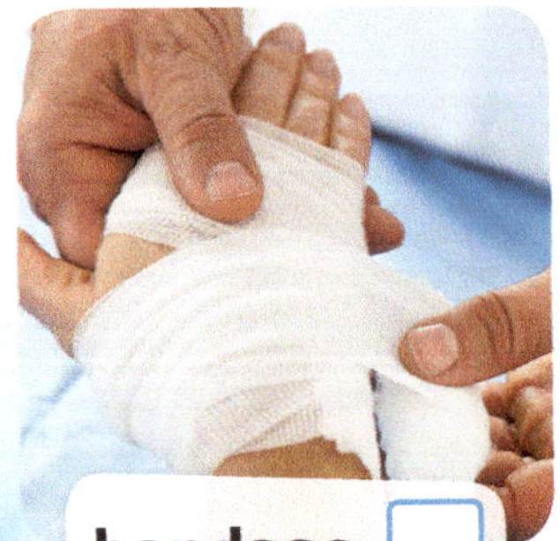

bandage ☐

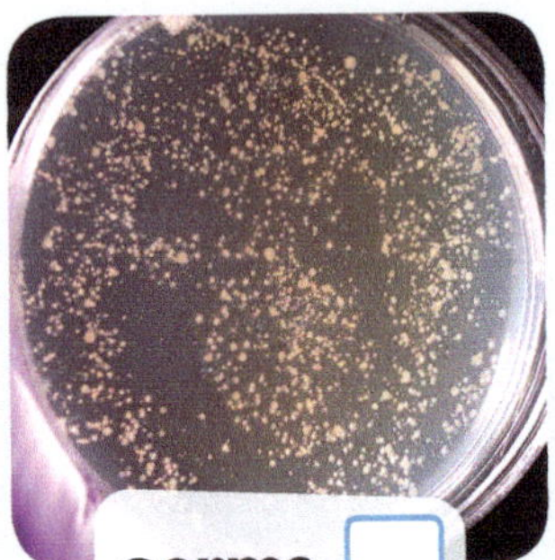

germs ☐

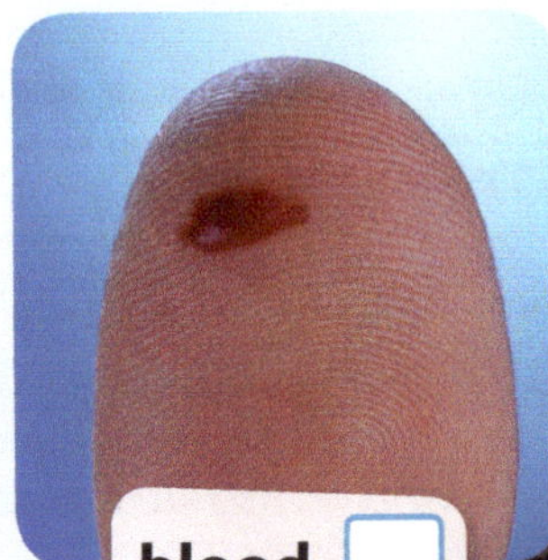

blood ☐

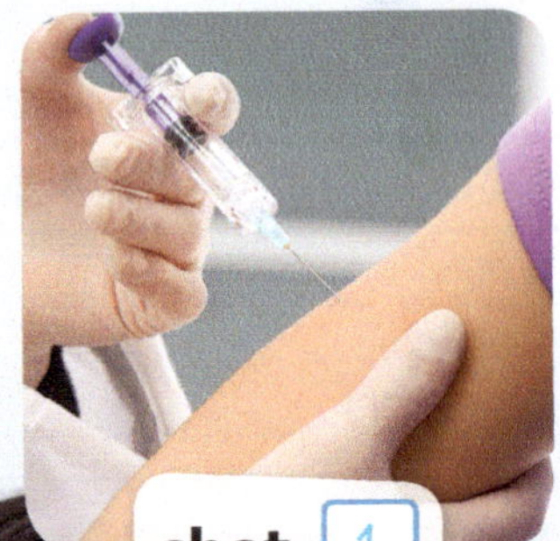

shot 1

nurse ☐

medicine ☐

clinic, shot

health centre, injection

B Listen, say, and number the pictures in **A**.

C Read and complete.

1 Sometimes when I'm sick, I have to take _medicine_ for a few days.

2 The ______________ gave me a ______________ in my arm.

3 I cut my finger yesterday, and there was a lot of ______________ .

4 My mom cleaned my finger and put a ______________ on it.

5 I have a ______________ . The doctor's going to put a ______________ on it.

D Now listen to Jorge and Olivia. Which museum has nurses' uniforms and hospital beds?

Jorge, Ecuador

Olivia, UK

E Listen again. Write *True* or *False*.

1 The museum in Quito has information about plants used as medicine. _True_

2 The Museum in Quito is in a new hospital. ______

3 There are old medical instruments at the museum in Quito. ______

4 Florence Nightingale was a famous doctor. ______

5 Florence Nightingale started a school for nurses. ______

6 At the museum in London, Olivia's class watched a play. ______

When do you see a doctor or nurse?
How can people stay healthy?

Explore Language

A Listen and read. How long was Heather sick?

Nurse Hayes:	Heather, how are you?
Heather:	I'm feeling better, thanks. I was sick for three days.
Nurse Hayes:	What was wrong?
Heather:	I had a fever. I was feeling hot and cold while I was helping you at the clinic. When I went home, I felt really sick.
Nurse Hayes:	Were you feeling sick while you were working with the children?
Heather:	A little. While we were working, I was washing my hands a lot.
Nurse Hayes:	Well, that's good!

B Look at **A**. Complete.

Past Progressive with *While*

I	was	______	hot and cold	______	I	______	helping you at the clinic.
______	you ______	sick	while	you	were	______	with the children?
While	we	______	______ ,	I	______	______	my hands.

Look

We use a comma after the *while* clause when it comes first.

C Think and discuss. Then choose.

1 We use *while* with the past progressive to talk about something that was happening at the same time as / after another action.

D Listen and say.

E Read and complete. Write about you.

1 While I was sleeping, my cat was playing with my toys .

2 We were eating dinner while ______________________.

3 While I was coming home from school, ______________________

______________________.

4 My classmates were making a lot of noise while ______________________

______________________.

5 While I was doing my homework, ______________________

______________________.

6 I was watching TV while ______________________.

F Play a chain game. What were you doing?

While you were sleeping, I was eating candy!

While she was sleeping and you were eating candy, I was swimming in the sea!

While she was sleeping and he was eating candy and you were swimming in the sea, I was climbing a mountain!

A Watch and listen. What is Natalia going to do?

Watch
How does Rania's body language show she is being kind to her friend?

B Watch again. Check (✔) the phrases you hear.

1. ✔ You don't look well.
2. ◯ I have a bad headache.
3. ◯ Oh, I'm sorry.
4. ◯ Let me give you some advice.
5. ◯ Are you drinking a lot of water?
6. ◯ Or you can buy a special cream.
7. ◯ I'm going to try taking a nap.
8. ◯ See you later!

Pronunciation /kw/ and /kr/

Listen and say.

quite   quiet   quickly   crash   crazy   cream

What other words do you know with these sounds?

C Plan. Choose two illnesses. Complete.

a broken leg | a cold | a cough | a stomachache | an earache | a fever | a sore throat

What's the matter?	I have ______.	→ Advice: ______
	I have ______.	→ ______

D Prepare your conversation. Use your ideas from **C** and sentences from **B**.

A Ask what's wrong

What's the matter?

B Say your illness

I have a ...

Ask a follow-up question

______

Respond

______

Give some advice

______

Thank your friend

______

E Practice with a friend.

Reflect
Was I kind to my friend?
Did I use different phrases to be kind?
Yes / No

Write About It

A Read the letter. Underline the simple past irregular verbs.

Tuesday, October 7th

Dear Alexis,

I'm sorry you're sick. I miss you a lot! Mr. Wolski said you have a bad cold. You should stay in bed and rest. Take some medicine, too. School was OK today, but it's more fun when you're here. We built volcanoes in our science class. Then, we went to the library. I found a great book about germs. I read it first, and then I gave it to Macio. Later, we had a rehearsal for the class play. Everybody knew the script! Mr. Wolski was surprised!

I felt really tired today. I slept badly last night. I think I had bad dreams.

I hope our letters help you feel better. Get well soon!

Your friend, Nasim

B Complete.

1 find → found
2 build → ______
3 know → ______
4 get → ______
5 read → ______
6 sleep → ______

Reflect
Did I use simple past verbs correctly?

C Plan. Think about writing a letter to a friend. Complete.

Greeting		Ask about your friend		Talk about your day		Talk about how you're feeling		Friendly closing
	→		→		→		→	

D Write your letter. Decorate it with pictures.

Read the questions and draw or write your answers.

What did I do?

What did I learn?

How did I learn?

How well did I do?

What can I do next?

Hello! I'm Nurse Hayes. What did you learn about staying healthy? Look for something huge in Unit 10!

UNIT 10 Don't Push the Button

A Listen and find. What does the machine make?

B Listen, say, and number the pictures in A.

C Close your eyes. Listen, visualize, and say.

TION DAY

D Look and write.

Parts of a machine	switch				
Actions					

E Listen and complete. Then watch and sing.

This Huge Machine

How do you work this huge machine?
It's easy! Watch and see what I mean.
You're right! It's easy! I see what you mean!

First, you 1 pull the lever and 2 f________ the switch,
Then, you 3 p________ the button and wait!
You 4 t________ the 5 g________ that turn the wheels
And fill the machine with paint!

Then the paper comes out and the colors are great,
And you pull the 6 l________ again.
The 7 w________ stop moving and the gears slow down,
And your time with the machine is at an end!

Explore Language

A Listen and read. What does Ting want to know?

B Look at **A**. Complete.

Comparatives with *Than* and *as … as*

This machine	______	even ______	______	the first one.
This little one		more ______		those big ones.

This machine	's	as	______	______	that house!
It	isn't	______	______	as	the big machines.

Watch Out

Comparatives use *than*, not ~~*then*~~.

C Think and discuss. Then choose.

1 We use *than* to say how two things are the same / different.

2 We use *as … as* to say how two things are the same / different.

D Listen and say.

E Look and complete.

1 The white gear is __as important as__ (important) the orange one.

2 The wheels on the elephant are ______________ (small) the wheels on the mouse!

3 The black gear is ______________ (big) the orange one.

4 The elephant is ______________ (complicated) the mouse.

5 The mouse is ______________ (simple) the elephant.

F Draw inventions and compare. How are they the same and different?

tall short long big small simple complicated interesting

My invention is bigger than yours.

Mine is more complicated.

Why do people invent new things?

A Listen to Lily talking to Grandpa José. What's special about his chair?

B Listen, say, and number the pictures in **A**.

C Read and complete.

1 My mom has shiny _gold_ and ________ jewelry.

2 My ________ T-shirt is cool and comfortable.

3 Our plates are easy to clean because they're made from ________ .

4 In winter, I wear my fuzzy ________ sweater and warm ________ gloves.

5 Pennies and nickels are made from different types of ________ .

6 We needed a lot of ________ for the fire.

D Now listen to Laura from Colombia. How old were the kids that she talks about?

Cassidy, USA

CJ, USA

E Listen again. Answer the questions.

1 What did Cassidy invent? _She invented crayon holders._

2 What is Cassidy's invention made of? ________

3 Why did Cassidy make her invention? ________

4 Who did CJ make videos for? ________

5 Who helped make CJ's first exercise video? ________

6 Where can you see CJ's videos? ________

What invention do you want to make?
Why is it important to share our ideas and inventions?

Explore Language

A Listen and read. What kind of wheels does the machine have?

Millie:	We have to move this machine to the gym today! Can it fit through the door?
Carla:	Yes, and I'm happy that we don't have to take it apart!
Millie:	The machine needs a switch to start and stop. Where could I put it?
Kareem:	You could put it there.
Millie:	No, I can't. There's no room.
Daniel:	What about this wheel?
Alec:	We shouldn't use plastic wheels. They aren't very strong. You should find a metal wheel.
Daniel:	OK, I think I see one.

B Look at **A**. Complete.

Modal Verbs

We	______	move this machine.	We	______	take it apart.
You	______	find a metal wheel.		______	use plastic wheels.
Where	______	I put it?	You	______	put it there.

The letter *l* is silent in *should* and *could*.

Watch out

C Think and discuss. Then choose.

1 We use *have to* / *could* when an action is necessary.

2 We use *have to* / *should* when we give advice.

3 We use *could* / *should* when we want to know if something is possible.

4 We use *don't have to* / *should* when an action is not necessary.

D Listen and say.

E Read and complete. Write about you.

1 At home, I have to help ______________________,
but I don't have to ______________________.

2 At school, we don't have to ______________________,
but we have to ______________________.

3 On the weekend, I shouldn't ______________________,
and I should ______________________.

4 Tonight, I could ______________________,
or I could ______________________.

F Play *Modal Madness*. Ask and answer about an imaginary machine.

Should I make a machine from gold and silver?

No, it's too expensive.

A Watch and listen. Who helped Lewis?

B Watch again. Check (✔) the phrases you hear.

1. ✔ I'm going to tell you a story about something I made.
2. ◯ This happened when I was in first grade.
3. ◯ I was seven years old.
4. ◯ Sometimes, I wanted to get away from them.
5. ◯ I made my own flag, too.
6. ◯ I loved my treehouse!
7. ◯ I made it myself!
8. ◯ It was my special place!

Pronunciation /br/ and /fl/

Listen and say.

branches breakfast bright flat floor flag

What other words do you know with these sounds?

C Plan. Think about something you made. Complete.

What did you make?	
When did you make it?	
Why did you make it?	
How did you make it?	
What happened?	

D Prepare your presentation. Use your ideas from **C** and phrases from **B**.

Introduction

I'm going to tell you a story about ...

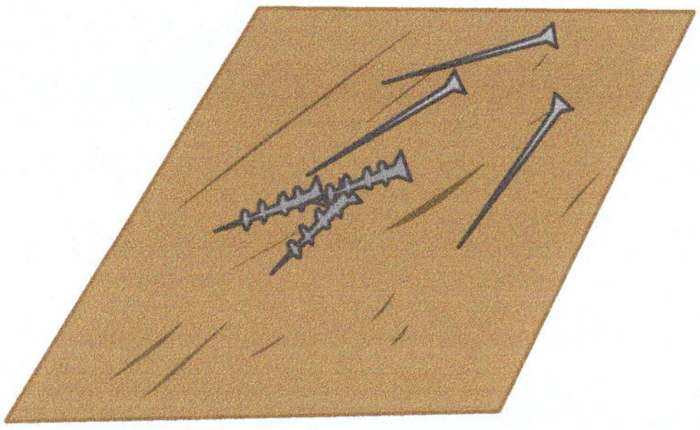

Middle

One day ...

Ending

E Practice with a friend. Then share with your class.

Reflect
Did I sound excited when I told my story?
Yes / No

Write About It

A Read the story. Circle the words that begin each paragraph.

Rainy Day Fun

One rainy day, Luiza was bored. She didn't want to read or play with her little brother. Then a truck came to the house. Two men brought in a new fridge for the kitchen. She watched the men take the fridge out of the box.

Suddenly, Luiza had an idea! First, Luiza cut the sides of the box carefully with scissors. Next, she opened the box up into a one flat piece of cardboard. Then, she took it to the top of the stairs and called her brother. It was a slide!

In the end, Luiza and her brother had fun all afternoon! Luiza loved her slide, and she made it herself!

B Look at A. Answer the questions.

1 What words begin the story? ______

2 What happens in the middle paragraph? ______

3 What words tell us about the order of events in the middle paragraph? ______

4 How does the writer begin the last paragraph? ______

C Plan a story about these three pictures. Write.

1 Beginning ______

2 Middle ______

3 End ______

Reflect
Did I use transition words to show the beginning, middle, and end of my story?

D Write your story.

Read the questions and draw or write your answers.

What did I do?

What did I learn?

ON

What was my favorite part?

How well did I do?

What can I do next?

UNIT 9

UNIT 10

Inside the Machine

HOW TO PLAY

1. Use your spinner to move around the board.
2. When you land on a square, answer the question or follow the instructions.
3. Ride up the gear, and slide down the pipe.
4. The winner is the first person to get to the finish.

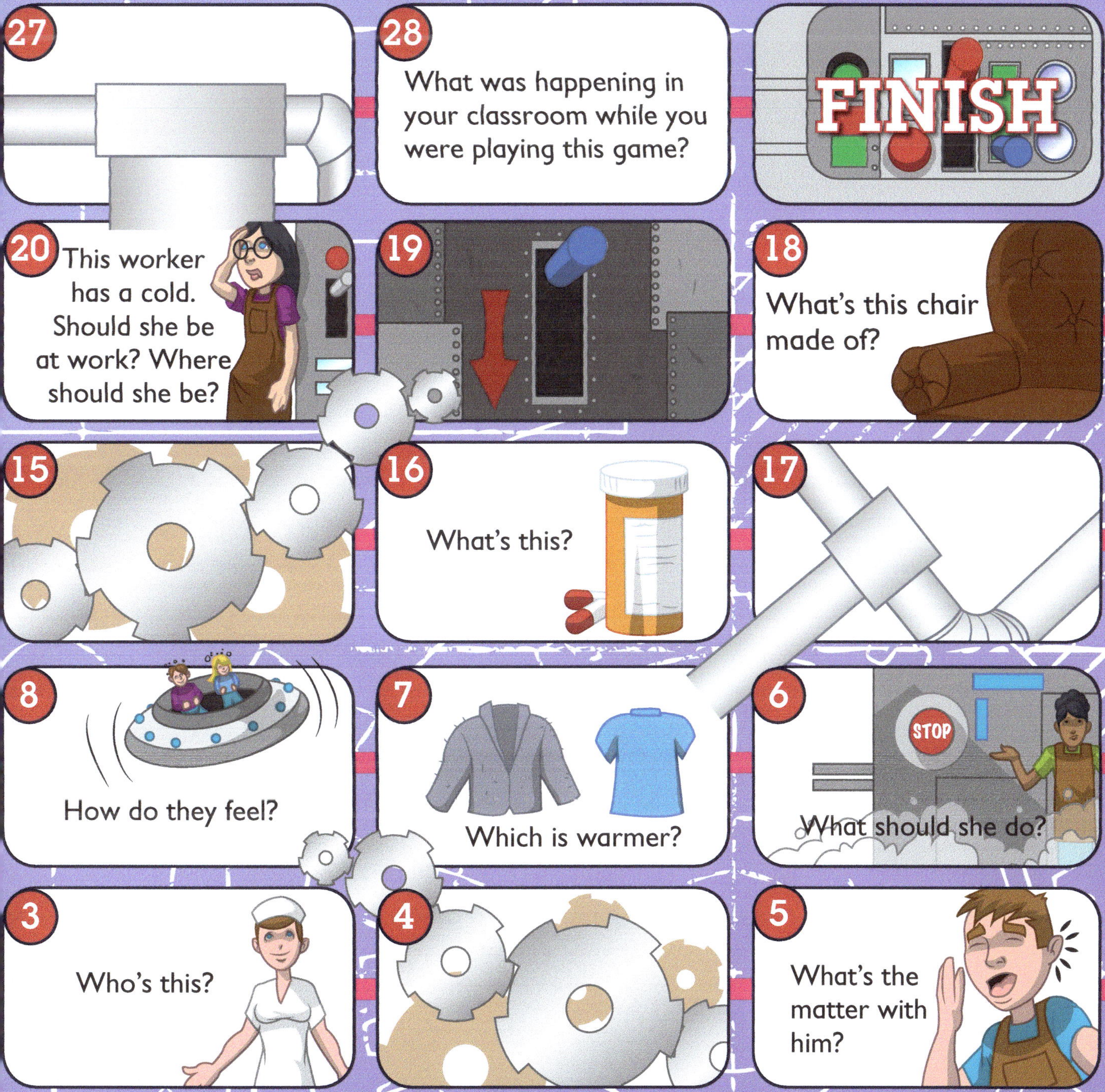

Play

The Grassland Orchestra

CHARACTERS

Faruk	Amelia
Marco	Isabella
Cheetah	Animals

Faruk, Amelia, and Isabella are at a table in the library. Marco looks at books on the shelves. He chooses a thick, old book and puts it on the table.

Marco: Look at this old book!
Faruk: It looks like a geography book.
Amelia: Could it be an adventure story?

Isabella opens the book. The four friends aren't in the library any more. The children fall off their chairs and onto the floor. Isabella holds the old book in her hands.

Faruk: What happened?
Amelia: I think we're in the book!

They stand up and look around.

Faruk: But where are we?
Isabella: We're in the grassland. The ground's covered with tall grass and flowers.

Marco: What was that crash?
Faruk: Look, a cheetah! Watch out! It's dangerous!

Cheetah comes running through the grass up to the children. They are afraid.

Cheetah: Hello! Don't be frightened. Many animals are more dangerous than I am.
Amelia: It's nice to meet you, Cheetah. Where are the other animals?
Cheetah: They're busy. You see, we have a complicated problem here. The grassland's very dry. We need water. So we're going to build a lake.
Isabella: Wow! Are lakes expensive?
Cheetah: Oh, yes. We need a million dollars—but we don't have any money.

Faruk: So, what are you going to do?
Cheetah: The Grassland Orchestra is going to have a performance! I'm the conductor, but I also play the cello.
Marco: I play the drums, and Isabella plays the piano. Can we help you?
Cheetah: Yes! Then you have to come to our rehearsal. We shouldn't be late.

Cheetah runs off and the children follow him. Finally, the rest of the orchestra arrives. They are all animals.

Cheetah: Hello, everyone! I'm glad you're on time. We have some new performers. They're going to join us. Let's tell them about the performance. When's it going to happen?
Animals: Tomorrow at noon!
Cheetah: Where are we going to perform?
Animals: On the stage!
Cheetah: How are we going to play?
Animals: Together! Loudly! Quietly! Quickly! Slowly! Proudly!
Cheetah: Right! Let's begin. Do you have your instruments?
Animals: Yes, we do!
Amelia: No, we don't.
Cheetah: WHAT? YOU DON'T HAVE YOUR INSTRUMENTS?
Marco: Well, we were reading …We weren't playing our instruments, …
Cheetah and **Animals:** ROAR!

The animals come towards the children angrily.

Amelia: Isabella, where's the book?
Isabella: Right here.
Faruk: Close it! Now!

Isabella closes the book. The children are back at their table in the library.

Isabella: That was exciting!

Marco goes back to the shelf and pulls out another book.

Marco: Let's try this science fiction book next.

Play

Into the Future

CHARACTERS

Noor
Kelsey
Jin
Laura
Diego
Chorus
Eli

Diego: Is this your time machine?
Jin: Yes. This is the machine that's going to take us into the future.
Diego: Cool! I'm ready.
Jin: What are you going to do in the future?
Diego: Me? I plan to look at sea life. I want to know about the coral reefs. Will people save them?
Jin: That's important. Go in!
Chorus: Thanks for coming. Step inside. Into the future! Let's go for a ride!

Diego enters the machine. Then, Noor walks over to the time machine. She is dressed as a doctor.

Jin: Hi, Noor! What are you going to do in the future?
Noor: I plan to talk to nurses and doctors. I want to find out about medicines that help people feel better.
Jin: Excellent plan! Go in.
Chorus: Thanks for coming. Step inside. Into the future! Let's go for a ride!

Noor enters the machine. Next, Eli comes over. He is dressed like a rescue worker and is carrying a big bag of tools.

Eli: Cool machine!
Jin: Thanks! I enjoyed building it. Why are you bringing all this?
Eli: I want to help rescue workers in the future. But what emergencies will I find? An earthquake, a hurricane, a forest fire? I have to be ready for everything!
Jin: Good luck! Go in.
Chorus: Thanks for coming! Step inside. Into the future! Let's go for a ride!

Eli brings all his tools into the machine. Then Laura appears. She is dressed like a chef.

Jin: Laura, what are your plans for the future?
Laura: I love cooking, so I want to learn about food in the future. What will people eat? Will they eat more protein? Will they still need to use a fridge or a stove?
Jin: That's interesting. Go in.
Chorus: Thanks for coming! Step inside. Into the future! Let's go for a ride!

Laura enters the machine. Jin looks around and checks the time.

Diego: Let's go, Jin!
Jin: But there's one more person who should be here …

Jin starts closing the door. Then, he sees Kelsey running toward him.

Kelsey: Wait!
Jin: You're late.
Kelsey: Sorry! I was walking through the park when a huge bird flew down and took my warm wool hat!
Jin: A bird took your hat?
Kelsey: Yes! I tried to catch it, but it flew faster and faster. And while it was flying, it was eating my hat! My hat's gone.
Jin: That's too bad. But we have to go now. Are you ready for the future?
Kelsey: Yes! I plan to study materials. I want to find out if people will still use things made from cotton or leather.
Jin: Sounds good! Go in.
Chorus: Thanks for coming. Step inside. Into the future! Let's go for a ride!

Kelsey starts to climb into the machine. Then she turns back to Jin.

Kelsey: Maybe I'll get a new hat!
Jin: Sorry, you can't bring things back from the future.
Kelsey: Hmmm … I think you're wrong. I'm going to bring something back!
Jin: What?
Kelsey: Ideas! We're all going to bring back ideas that will save the world!

Kelsey and Jin both enter the machine. Jin pulls a lever and the door closes He pushes a button that says START.

Chorus: We stepped inside! Into the future! We're going for a ride!

Macmillan Education
4 Crinan Street
London N1 9XW
A division of Springer Nature Limited

Companies and representatives throughout the world

Language Book ISBN 978-1-786-32874-8
Student Book Pack ISBN 978-1-380-00235-8

Written by Shelagh Speers

The author has asserted her right to be identified as the author of this work in accordance with the Copyright, Designs and Patents Act 1988.

First published 2019

Original design by D'Sign Lab
Page make-up by Pronk
Illustrated by Emiliano Ordás: 6-9, 140-143; Barbara Cantini (Lemonade Illustration Agency): 10-13, 16, 18-19, 20-21; Rob Foote (Beehive Illustration): 22-24, 27-28, 30-35; Jennifer Zivoin (MB Artists): 36-39, 42-47; Maine Diaz (MB Artists): 48-50, 54, 56, 59-61; Gustavo Mazali (Beehive Illustration): 62-65, 68-73; Irina Golina-Sagatelian (Beehive Illustration): 69; Marta Comito (Lemonade Illustration Agency): 74-77, 80, 82-83, 85-87; Guy Wolek (Blasco Agency): 88-90, 94, 96-97, 99; Abigail Dela Cruz (Lemonade Illustration Agency): 100-102, 106, 108-109, 111-113; Arpad Olbey (Beehive Illustration): 114-116, 120, 122-125; Kevin Myers (Lemonade Illustration Agency): 126-129, 132, 134-139.
Front cover design and concept by 3CD
Cover adaptation by Roberto Martinez
Cover photographs by **Getty Images**/Leonello Calvetti (globe), Getty Images/Kinzie Riehm (girl).
Picture research by Penelope Bowden, Proudfoot Pictures

Author's acknowledgements
Grateful thanks to my husband Greg and daughter Laura for their love and encouragement. I dedicate this book to all the authors I have worked with—they are my inspiration.

The publishers would like to thank: Viv Lambert and Mo Choy, Salwa Abid, Meryem Bennis, Leticia Blázquez, Angel Bonilla, Victor Cojulun, John Cruft, Silvia Díez de Rivera, Randa Farouk, Magda Giomazi, Vangelina Hernández, Quyen Ho, Ziad Jadallah, Youngkwang Jang, Faisal M'reish, Riham Almughrabi, Jackie Mustoe, Adriana Ochoa, Devrim Ozdemir, Maria Pia Ayala, Silvia Raya, Ola Refaat, Helen Sharbain, Sana Sifri, Esra Tosun, Lemmy Trujillo, Tamer Victor, Jake Whiddon, Sandra Wu, Amanda Zhang, Colegio Buckingham and Gabriela Rodríguez, Colegio Euterpe and Angélica Sánchez, Colegio Héroes Mexicanos and Marcelo Carlos Hernández Morales, Internaciones Campus Fraijanes and Ana Monica Thomas, New Victoria International College and Ghada Hassan Mokbel, The Southern Cross School and Dayana Acevedo, Antonia Lira, and Paula Jorquera, Verbo Quetzaltenango and Cindy Steicy Ixchiu Velásquez

The author and publishers would like to thank the following for permission to reproduce their photographs: **123RF**/Brent Hofacker p78(br), 123RF/TAKASHI HONMA p130(cl), 123RF/Sakarin Sawasdinaka p78(bl), 123RF/Carlo Villa p118(tm); **Alamy**/Andy Dean Photography p104(main image), Alamy/Everett Collection Historical p119(r) Alamy/Malcolm Fairman p66(tml), Alamy/Gabbro p119(l), Alamy/Jiri Hubatka p66(bl), Alamy/Warinthorn Krueangkham p26(cl), Alamy/Konstantin Labunskiy p131(r), Alamy/Anton Prado p118(cm), Alamy/SJA Photo p26(cr), Alamy/Nature Photographers Ltd/PAUL R. STERRY p26(tml), Alamy/Jochen Tack p105(l),Alamy/WaterFrame p113(2), Alamy/Wavebreak Media ltd p118(main image), Alamy/XenLights p52(cml); **FLPA**/Chris Newbert/Minden Pictures p104(tml); **Getty Images** p112(4), Getty Images/Martin Barraud p40(main image), Getty Images/Thomas Barwick p67(l), Getty Images/Garry Black p26(tmr), Getty Images/Blend Images p92(girl inset), Getty Images/blue jean images p53(l), Getty Images/BSIP/UIG p118(tcr), Getty Images/Peter Cade p14(cm), Getty Images/cometary p41(l), Getty Images/Daisy-Daisy p92(main image), Getty Images/JAG IMAGES p41(r), Getty Images/Jamie Grill Photography p118(tl), Getty Images/Furtseff p66(tl), Getty Images/gegeonline p92(bmr), Getty Images/greenlin p52(bml), Getty Images/Anna Gorin pp92(cmr), 112(10), Getty Images/Jamie Grill p14(tcr), Getty Images/Julien Grondin p92(tcr), Getty Images/GUSTOIMAGES/SCIENCE PHOTO LIBRARY p78(tcr), Getty Images/Hhakim p113(8), Getty Images/hakoar p26(tl), Getty Images/Claire-Marie Harris p79(l), Getty Images/Dan Herrick pp104(bmr), 113(5), Getty Images/Nico Hermann p15(l), Getty Images/Hero Images pp14(main image, 52cr), Getty Images/Hill Street Studios pp52(t), 66(main image), Getty Images/Steven Hunt pp104(tmr), 113(1), Getty Images/LIU JIN/Stinger p105(r), Getty Images/Jupiterimages p14(br), Getty Images/kali9 p52(cmr), Getty Images/Keenpress p26(b), *Getty Images/Steven_Kriemadis p52(bl Getty Images/LatitudeStock -* Mel Longhurst p14(bl), Getty Images/John Lund pp92(cml), 104(br), 113(11), Getty Images/Maximilian Stock Ltd. p14(bmr), Getty Images/Medioimages/Photodisc p112(12), Getty Images/Eric Meola p92(tornado), Getty Images/Kerstin Meyer p104(tr), Getty Images/Mint Images - Frans Lanting p92(bcr), Getty Images/NiklasEmmoth p131(l), Getty Images/OlafSpeier p66(bmr), Getty Images/pixelfusion3d p15(r), Getty Images/Tim Platt p67(r), Getty Images/PrairieArtProject p93(r), Getty Images/Purestock p14(bml), Getty Images/H. Armstrong Roberts/ClassicStock p66(bml), Getty Images/rusm pp40(tl, tml, tmr, tr), Getty Images/Nestor Sakelliou/FOAP p92(br), Getty Images/Luis Fernando Sanchez-Moreno Fdez/EyeEm p66(cml), Getty Images/Sean3810 p93(l), Getty Images/Tristan Savatier p130(tcr), Getty Images/Thomas M. Scheer/EyeEm p130(tr), Getty Images/STEEX p14(bcr), Getty Images/Stephen Simpson Inc p130(main image), Getty Images/Larry Washburn p66(tr), Getty Images/Jolien Weytens/EyeEm p26(cml),Getty Images/wrangle p112(6), Getty Images/yotrak p52(bmr), Getty Images/a3701027 p92(tr); **Glow Images**/Blend RF p92(bl), Glow Images/Deposit Photos p78(tr); **Nature Picture Library**/Bernard Castelein p27(l), Nature Picture Library/Brandon Cole p104(bml), Nature Picture Library/Sue Daly p104(bcl), Nature Picture Library/Georgette Douwma p104(bl), Nature Picture Library/Neil Lucas p27(r), Nature Picture Library/Tony Wu p104(tl); **Powerstock** p112(3);Robert Harding/Pierre Lobel p113(7); **Shutterstock**/135pixels p79(r), Shutterstock/Africa Studio p66(tmr), Shutterstock/Aha-Soft pp40(bcm, bcr, br), Shutterstock/kirillov alexey p26(cmr), Shutterstock/Kitch Bain p52(br), Shutterstock/RUI FERREIRA p40(tcr), Shutterstock/Deyan Georgiev p53(r), Shutterstock/goodluz p14(tr), Shutterstock/ifong p78(bcr), Shutterstock/Jiri Hera p40(tcm), Shutterstock/lauro55 p66(br), Shutterstock/Nalaphotos p26(tr), Shutterstock/Nina.G p130(tcl), Shutterstock/Pete Pahham p136, Shutterstock/Andrey_Popov p118(tr), Shutterstock/puhhha p78(main image), Shutterstock/Hasan Shaheed p58, Shutterstock/sumire8 p130(tl), Shutterstock/SOKUR SVITLANA p130(cr), Shutterstock/Dave Weaver p92(bml), Shutterstock/Y Photo Studio p78(bmr), Shuuterstock/Andfei Zveaghintev p112(9); **Science Photo Library**/CROWN COPYRIGHT/HEALTH & SAFETY LABORATORY p118(cl).

Printed and bound in Uruguay

2023
30

Global Stage

Literacy Book 3

Katie Foufouti and Paul Mason

macmillan education

Scope and Sequence

Unit	Reading 1	Reading 2	Reading Skill	Content Area	Social and Emotional Learning	Key Concept	Language Book
Literacy Review	Scanning; Identifying Cause and Effect; Sequence of Events;; Final *st* and Initial *tr*; Identifying the Main Idea and Details; Identifying Fact and Opinion; Final *nd* and *ng*						
1 I Love Reading page 8	**Fiction** *The Beginning of Alice's Adventures* Fantasy	**Nonfiction** *Learning and Your Brain* Informational Text **Spelling** final *er*	Skimming a text	Science: Neuroscience	Self-Awareness: Label and recognize own and others' emotions	Why is reading important?	**Vocabulary** book genres and adjectives, school subjects **Grammar** simple past review, regular and irregular verbs, adverbs of manner
2 What Lives Here? page 24	**Nonfiction** *Two Different Forests* Informational Text	**Fiction** *A New Friend* Folk Tale **Spelling** *ai*	Understanding the author's purpose	Science: Ecology	Responsible Decision-Making: Make decisions based on moral, personal, and ethical standards	How are plants, animals, and humans connected?	**Vocabulary** plants, animals, and nature **Grammar** comparatives and superlatives with adjectives and adverbs
3 How Much Is It? page 40	**Nonfiction** *The History of Money* Informational Text	**Fiction** *The $100 Bill* Story **Spelling** *ar*	Identifying problems and solutions	History: Culture	Responsible Decision-Making: Identify problems when making decisions, and generate alternatives	Why do we need money?	**Vocabulary** money and math **Grammar** modals: *have to/ don't have to, should/shouldn't, could*
4 We Can Do It page 56	**Nonfiction** *Teamwork Makes the Dream Work* Informational Text **Spelling** *or*	**Fiction** *Late for the Show* Play	Understanding the sequence of events	Social Studies: Teamwork	Relationship Skills: Exhibit cooperative learning and working toward group goals	How does teamwork help us?	**Vocabulary** theater and time **Grammar** past progressive
5 Make Some Noise page 72	**Nonfiction** *The Art of Sound* Informational Text **Spelling** *ou*	**Fiction** *Beethoven's 9th* Poem	Understanding cause and effect	Arts & Humanities: Music	Social Awareness: Respect others	What different types of sounds are in our world?	**Vocabulary** sounds and musical instruments **Grammar** *going to* for making plans

Unit	Reading 1	Reading 2	Reading Skill	Content Area	Social and Emotional Learning	Key Concept	Language Book
6 That Looks Good page 88	**Fiction** *Little Chef* Story	**Nonfiction** *Too Young to Cook? True Stories of Young Chefs* Persuasive Text **Spelling** final *old*	Scanning for specific information	Arts & Humanities: Culinary Arts	Responsible Decision-Making: Implement problem-solving skills when making decisions, when appropriate	Why is food important?	**Vocabulary** kitchen and food **Grammar** verb patterns with infinitives and gerunds
7 How Can We Help? page 104	**Fiction** *What Happens Next?* Story	**Nonfiction** *Animals to the Rescue* Informational Text **Spelling** final *ly*	Making inferences and predictions	Social Studies: Communities	Self-Management: Exhibit positive motivation, hope, and optimism	How can we help each other in a disaster?	**Vocabulary** emergencies and natural disasters **Grammar** relative clauses with *who* and *that*
8 Under the Sea page 120	**Nonfiction** *Coral Reefs* Persuasive Text **Spelling** final *ight*	**Fiction** *The Lost Camera* Fantasy	Identifying perspective	Science: Marine Biology	Social Awareness: Identify social cues (verbal, physical) to determine how others feel	What is life like under the sea?	**Vocabulary** sea life and appearance **Grammar** simple present review, present progressive review, future with *will*
9 What's the Matter? page 136	**Nonfiction** *Take Your Medicine* Informational Text **Spelling** *ur*	**Fiction** *A Surprise Cure* Story	Understanding the main idea and details	Science: Health & Medicine	Self-Management: Set plans and work toward goals	What do we do when we're sick?	**Vocabulary** illness and treatment **Grammar** simple past and past progressive with *when* review, past progressive with *while*
10 Don't Push the Button page 152	**Nonfiction** *Moving Machines* Informational Text	**Fiction** *Searching for Sterling* Science Fiction **Spelling** *ough*	Understanding facts and opinions	Science: Engineering	Self-Management: Overcome obstacles and create strategies for more long-term goals	Does technology make our lives easier?	**Vocabulary** machines and materials **Grammar** comparatives review, modals review

A Scan the story. Answer the questions. Then listen and read.

1 What is the title? ______

2 What is the setting? ______

3 Who are the characters? ______

Don't Move

A strong wind blew through the trees and our tent shook like a sail. Mom and I were the only two people out on the forest trail that night. I felt very alone. I wished we were at home and I was sleeping in my own bed.

"Camping out here will be worth it, Suzie," Mom said with a smile. "We'll get some amazing butterfly photos in the morning."

Just then, from outside the thin walls of the tent, I heard a grunting noise. I jumped. It was some kind of animal. The creature started moving around the tent. One moment, the grunting was next to our heads. Then, it was by our feet.

"What is it?" I whispered.

"It's looking for food. Stay close," said Mom. "And don't move."

B Read and write *True* or *False*.

1 Mom and Suzie are sleeping in a hut on a mountain. False

2 It is a calm and peaceful night. ______

3 Mom and Suzie are in the forest to take butterfly photos. ______

4 They hear a grunting sound from outside the tent. ______

5 The creature moves around the tent. ______

C Read, think, and write.

Cause		Effect
1 A strong wind blew.	▶	______
2 ______	▶	Suzie felt very alone.
3 Suzie heard a grunting noise.	▶	______
4 ______	▶	The creature moved around the tent.

D Put the events in order.

- [ ] The creature started moving around the tent.
- [1] A strong wind blew through the trees and our tent shook like a sail.
- [ ] Just then, from outside the thin walls of the tent, I heard a grunting noise.
- [ ] "Camping out here will be worth it, Suzie," Mom said with a smile.
- [ ] "It's looking for food. Stay close," said Mom. "And don't move."

My Reading Journal

What do you think happens next? Write.

______

______

______

______

Phonics *–st and tr–*

Listen and unscramble. Then find more words ending with *st* and beginning with *tr* in the reading.

1 staf	fast	5 ashtr	______
2 aintr	______	6 tseb	______
3 enst	______	7 tirfs	______
4 avtrel	______	8 uret	______

A Scan the reading. Answer the questions. Then listen and read.

1 Which city is close to the forest? ____________

2 What is the species of butterfly? ____________

3 How far do some of the butterflies travel? ____________

The Monarch Butterfly's Journey

Every fall, in the mountains about 97 km. northwest of Mexico City, something amazing happens. Millions of monarch butterflies arrive at the same small part of the forest. Some monarch butterflies travel more than 4,000 km. from North America to escape the winter and to mate.

Every year in this forest, there are so many butterflies that the trees turn orange. Branches bend under the weight. In spring, the forest fills with the fluttering of tiny wings, as the monarchs get ready to make the long journey back home.

Every fall, monarch butterflies travel south.

This part of the forest is now a UNESCO World Heritage Site. Scientists believe this place is important for the planet and for the monarch butterfly species. People take care of this forest. The trees here cannot be cut down.

B Read and answer.

1 When do the monarch butterflies arrive in Mexico?

The butterflies arrive in Mexico every fall.

2 Where do the monarch butterflies travel from?

____

3 How far is the forest from Mexico City?

____

4 What happens to the trees because of the butterflies?

____

5 When do the monarchs start their journey back home?

____

C Think and write. What is the main idea? What are the details?

Main Idea		
Detail	Detail	Detail

D Read and write *Fact* or *Opinion*.

1 The monarch butterflies are the most beautiful in the world. Opinion

2 Millions of monarch butterflies migrate to Mexico each year. ______

3 It really is so amazing to see the butterflies. ______

4 Some monarch butterflies travel more than 4,000 km. ______

5 The forest is protected. ______

My Reading Journal

What's one thing you learned from the reading?

____

Phonics *–nd and –ng*

Listen and complete with *nd* and *ng*. Then find more words ending with *nd* and *ng* in the reading.

1 se n d
2 fi __ __
3 sta __ __
4 wro __ __
5 thi __ __
6 si __ __
7 stro __ __
8 sou __ __

UNIT 1 I Love Reading

Question Starts

A Think about the picture. Then brainstorm questions. Write a list.

Who What Where
When Why How

B Look at your list from **A**. Which questions seem the most interesting? Discuss them with the class.

What book is she reading?

Where is she?

C What new ideas or questions do you have now? Talk about your ideas with your partner.

How many books are there in the whole world?

Is there a country in the world without a library?

D Think and discuss. How does reading take us to other times and places?

E Look quickly at the story on the next page, but don't read all the words. Answer the questions.

1 How does Alice feel?

____

2 What kind of animal does she see?

____

Now read **The Beginning of Alice's Adventures**

Fiction

The Beginning of Alice's Adventures

Alice sat by the river. Her sister read a novel. Alice was bored and hot. She felt sleepy, and she wondered what to do.

vest

waistcoat

What do you think *Goodness me!* means?

Suddenly, a rabbit ran past her. The rabbit was white with pink eyes. He wore a yellow waistcoat.

"Goodness me!" said Alice. "What's that? A rabbit in a waistcoat!" She was very surprised. "Rabbits don't wear waistcoats!"

Lewis Carroll wrote *Alice's Adventures in Wonderland* in 1865. Today, it's in more than 170 languages!

The rabbit stopped and took a watch out of his pocket.

"Oh dear, oh dear, I'm going to be late," he said. The rabbit ran off.

Words in Context

Find these words in the reading. What do you think they mean?

sleepy   chased   fell   shelves   corner

Alice got up, quickly, and chased after him.

The rabbit jumped down a very big hole. Alice jumped in after him.

Imagine you fell through the Earth. Where would you land?

Alice fell—down, down, down—for a very long time.

As she fell, Alice could see shelves of interesting books and things on the sides of the hole.

"I wonder if I'm near the center of the Earth," she said.

Down, down, down.

"I might go right through the Earth and end up in New Zealand," said Alice. She knew all about the geography of the Earth from school.

center

centre

Then, suddenly—*thump*! Alice landed at the bottom of the hole. She saw the White Rabbit run around the corner.

Alice ran after him as fast as she could.

Alice came to a room full of doors. But where was the White Rabbit? She couldn't see him, and all the doors were locked.

Then Alice saw a little golden key on a table. She picked it up. "I wonder which door this key opens?"

This was just the beginning of Alice's exciting adventures in Wonderland. But she didn't know that!

Did the adventure really happen, or did Alice imagine it?

Explore the Reading

A Read and number. Put the events in order.

- [ ] Alice came to a room full of doors and found a little golden key.
- [ ] Alice fell down the hole. She fell for a long time.
- [ ] Alice sat by the river with her sister.
- [ ] The rabbit jumped down a large hole. Alice jumped in, too.
- [ ] Alice landed at the bottom of the hole.
- [ ] A white rabbit ran past Alice.

B Look and write. How do they feel?

worried   bored   ~~surprised~~   interested

1

surprised

2

______

3

______

4

______

C Think and discuss. Do you have a big imagination like Alice? What do you imagine?

> Yes, I do. Sometimes, I imagine ...

A Read quickly. Don't read all the words. Write three important pieces of information. Then discuss.

Then, Alice saw a little door about 38 cm. high. She tried the little golden key in the lock, and it fit! She was very happy!

Alice opened the door carefully. It led into a lovely garden. She really wanted to explore the garden and look at the beautiful flowers … but she couldn't get her head through the door. "Oh, no, I can't go into the garden. I'm too big!" she said sadly.

38 centimeters = 15 inches

1 ______

2 ______

3 ______

When we **skim**, we look at the reading quickly and don't read every word. We look for important information, important words, at titles, and at captions to understand the main idea.

B Skim *Learning and Your Brain* on the next page. What is it about? Check (✔).

1 The size of the brain. ◯

2 The different parts of the brain we use when we learn. ◯

3 What the brain looks like. ◯

4 What the imagination is. ◯

C Think and discuss. What do you know about the brain? What does the brain do?

The brain is …

It can …

Now read **Learning and Your Brain**

Nonfiction

Learning and Your Brain

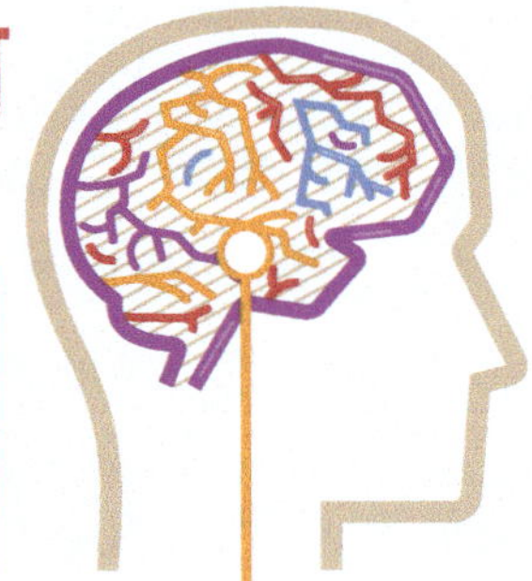

The Lobes of the Brain

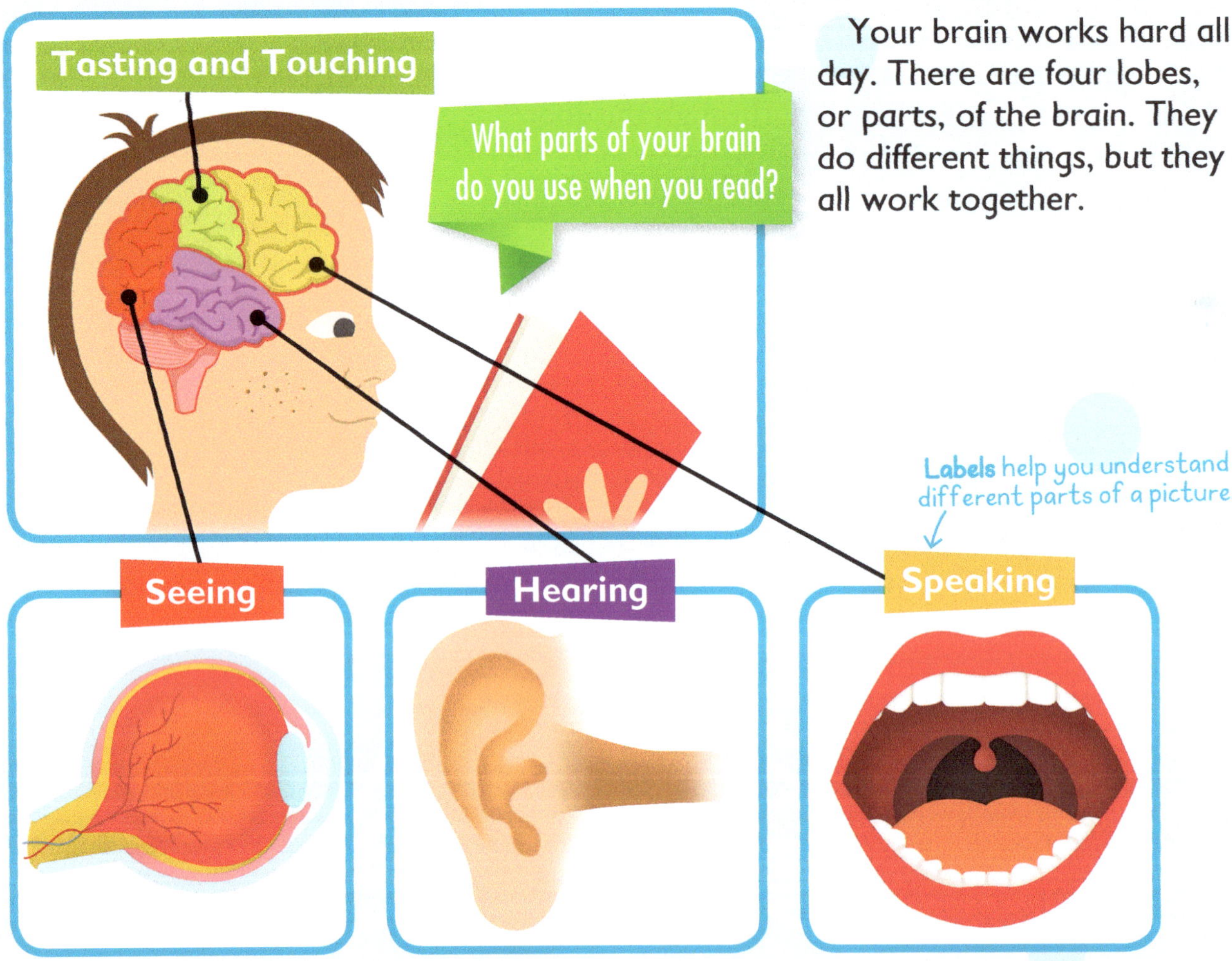

Your brain works hard all day. There are four lobes, or parts, of the brain. They do different things, but they all work together.

Part of your brain helps you understand what you taste and touch. Can you find it? Another part of your brain helps you see. Can you find it?

When your teacher reads to you, part of your brain helps you hear the words. It also works when you read silently. Can you find it? Part of your brain helps you speak. It also helps you understand what you are reading. Can you find it?

When you do different things, the lobes of your brain work together like a team. Using the different parts makes them stronger. Reading is a good way to exercise your brain and give it a workout.

Hearing Words

Seeing Words

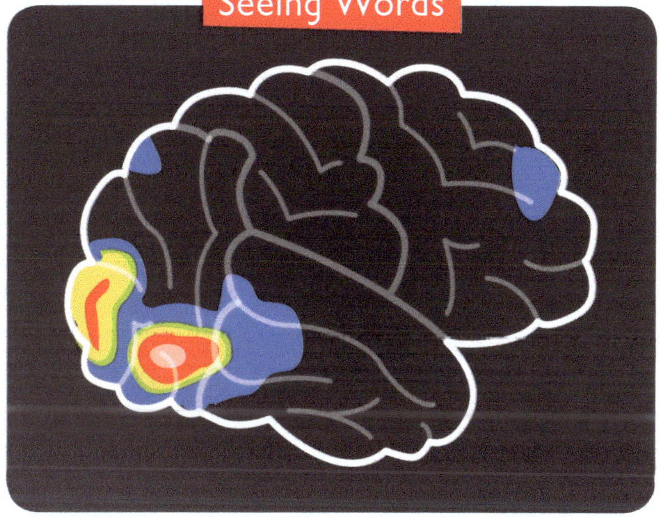

Speaking Words

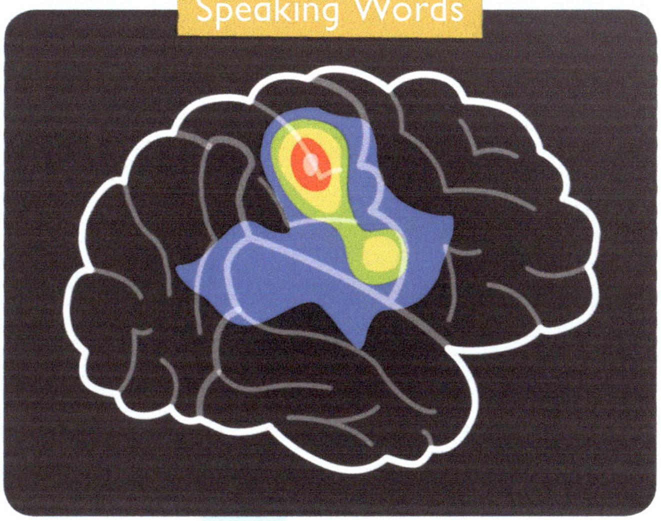

Thinking About Words

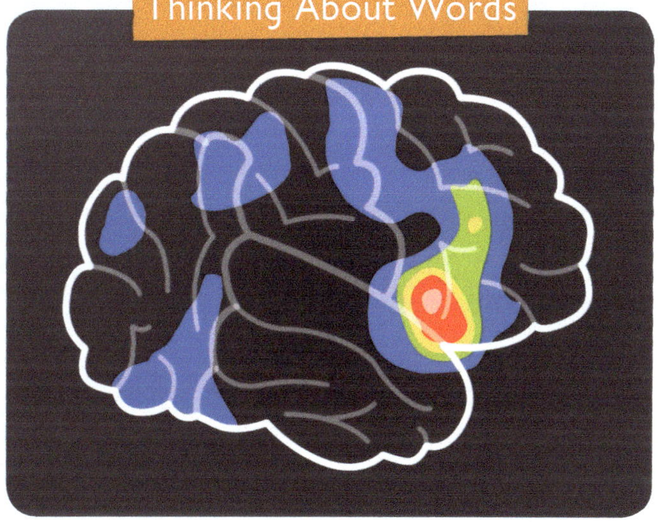

Scientists use a special machine to see which parts of the brain we use at different times. During each activity, the red areas show the parts we're using the most, the blue areas show the parts we're using a little bit, and the black areas show parts we aren't using much at all.

Words in Context

Find these words in the reading. What do you think they mean?

lobes workout cells fibers
messages connecting creative

Neurons Make Connections

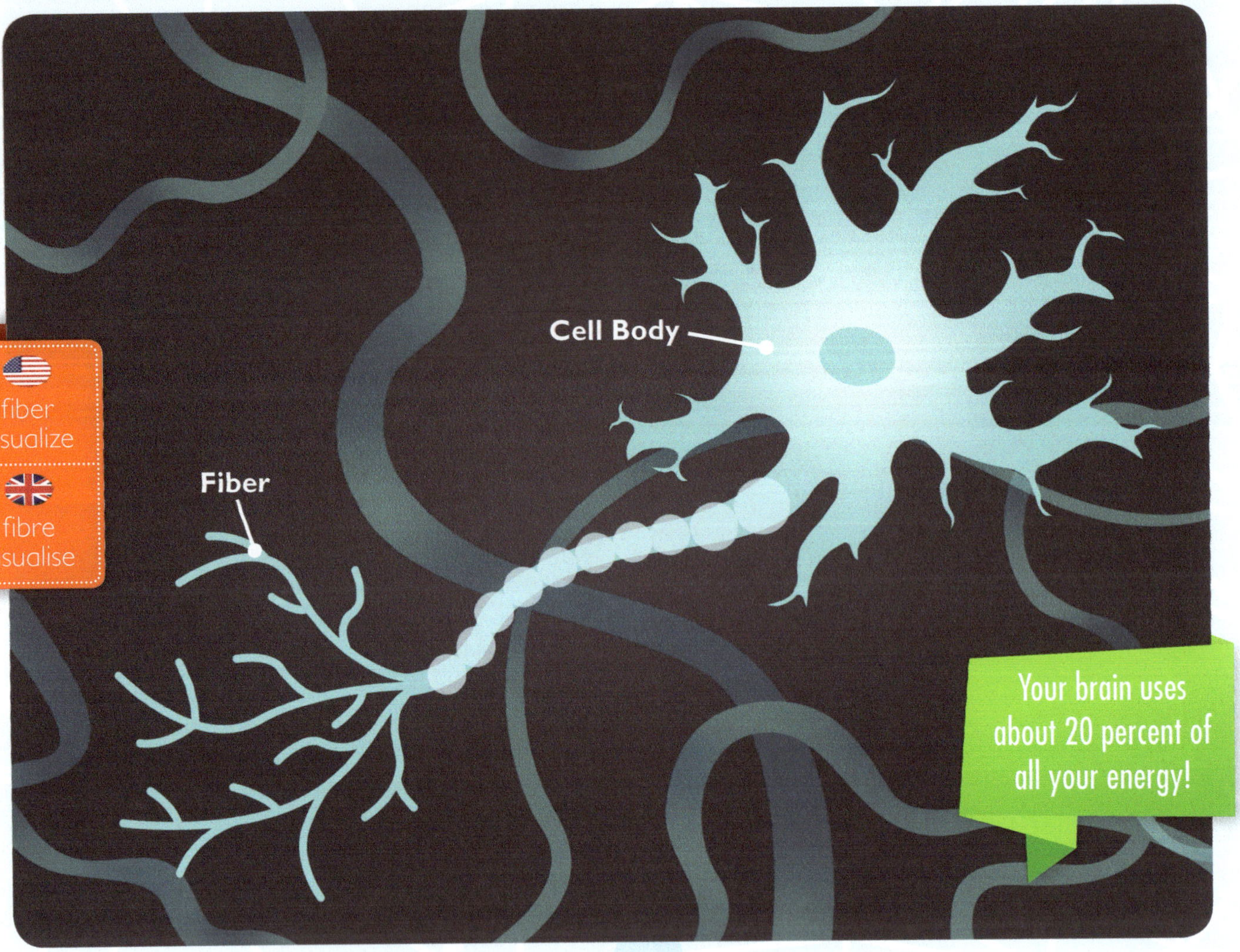

fiber
visualize

fibre
visualise

Your brain is made up of billions of special cells called neurons. Each neuron has a body with fibers that look like the branches of a tree. These fibers join together, connecting neurons so they can send each other messages or information.

The more you read, the stronger these connections become.

Reading Helps Your Imagination

When you read, your brain helps you visualize, or imagine, what the story might look like. Scientists think reading improves the imagination because it makes the connections in our brains stronger. This makes us more creative.

Your Brain and Other Subjects

In P.E., you run and kick a ball. Goal! You use this part of your brain.

How much is 1 + 1 + 1 + 1 + 1? What about 10 − 1? How about 2 × 2? This part of the brain helps you solve math problems.

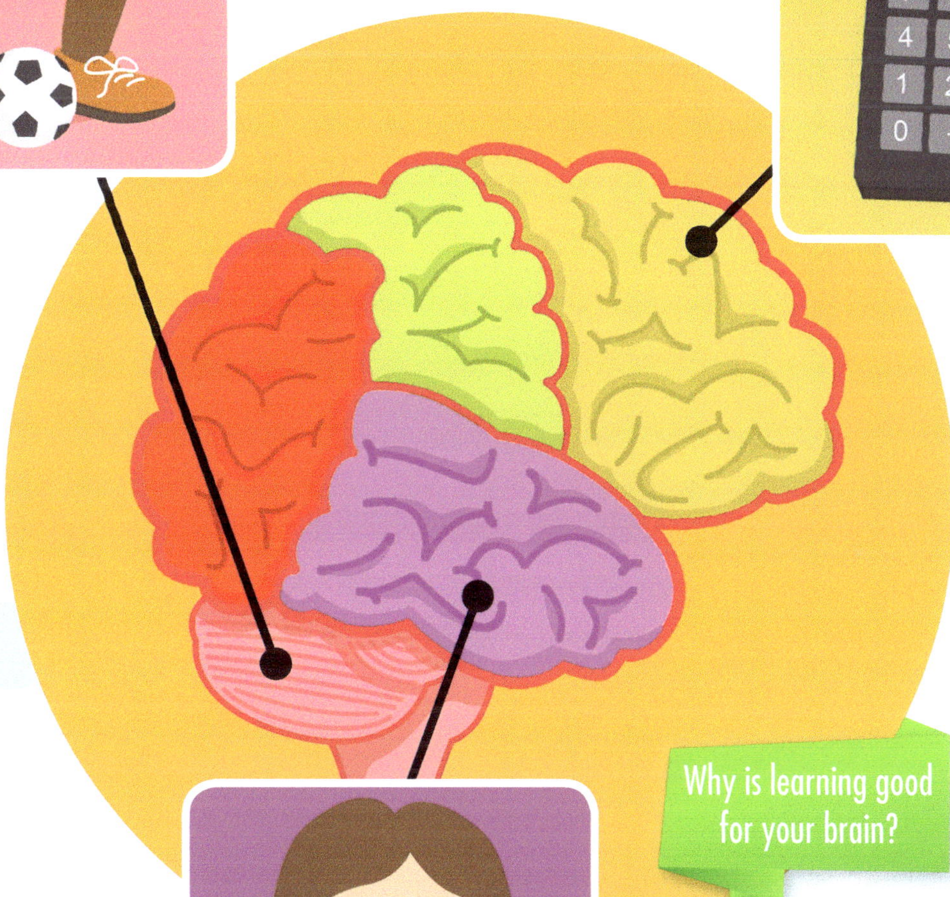

When you listen to music, this part of your brain is working.

Keep reading and learning to keep your brain in good shape.

Explore the Reading

A Write *True* or *False*. Say the page where you found the answer.

1 The brain is made up of billions of special cells called imagination cells. ______
2 Your brain uses 20 percent of your body's energy! ______
3 To help you read, different parts of the brain work together. ______
4 Scientists think reading improves your imagination. ______
5 Reading and learning don't keep your brain in good shape. ______

B Read and color the parts of the brain.

purple = You listen to music.
red = You see words.
yellow = You speak.
green = You taste an apple.

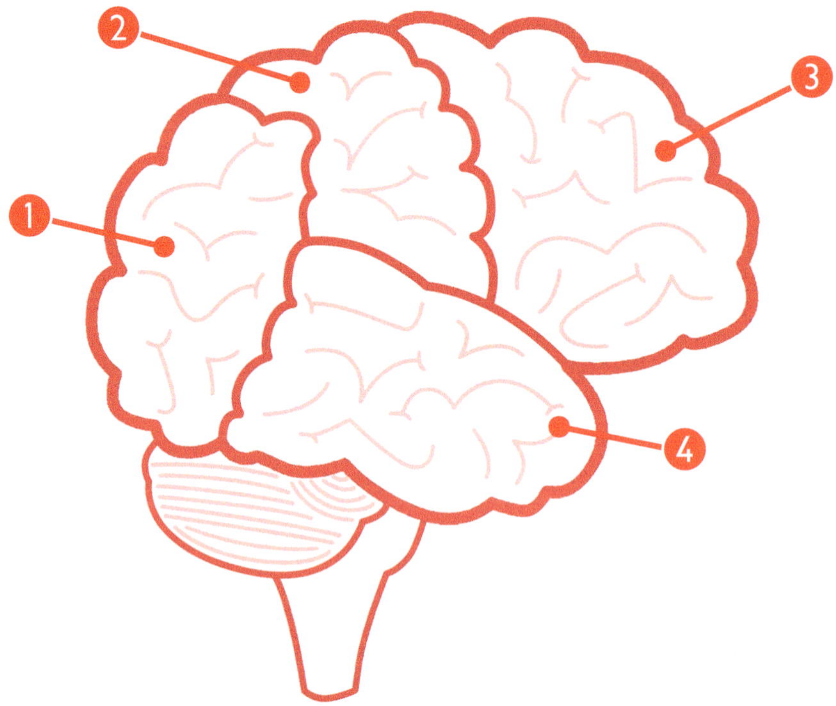

C Think and discuss. Do you give your brain a good workout?

Yes, I read ...

Spelling Pattern –*er*

Listen and write. Then check your answers.

1 c______ 2 w______ 3 a______ 4 f______ 5 r______

Now find more words ending with *er* in the reading.

Why is reading important?

A What different types of things do we read? Why do we read them? Complete the table.

What We Read …	And Why We Read It!
The Beginning of Alice's Adventures	for fun
Learning and Your Brain	for information

B Think and write. Why is it important to read different things?

Reasons to Read

You can learn new facts. ______________________

____

____

____

C Discuss your ideas. Then share with your class. Do a Numbered Heads Together routine.

I think it's important because ...

My Reading Journal

Did you like the fiction or the nonfiction reading better? Why? Write.

I liked the ______________ reading better, because ______________________.

Color the rabbits to rate the unit. Then write a short review.

I thought this unit was ______________________

____

UNIT 2

What Lives Here?

See, Think, Wonder

A Look at the picture. What do you see?

I see a river.

I see cameras.

B What do you think?

I think they like animals.

The bear is friendly.

C What do you wonder?

Why are they taking pictures?

Is it cold there?

D Think and discuss. What kinds of plants and animals do you have in your area? What do they look like?

E Read and check. These two headings are from the article. Why do you think the author used them?

Deciduous Forests **Coniferous Forests**

1 To explain why coniferous trees are better than deciduous forests. ◯

2 To compare two types of forest. ◯

3 To describe the trees that grow nearby. ◯

Now read **Two Different Forests**

Nonfiction

Two Different Forests

Deciduous Forests

← Headings tell us what the reading is going to be about.

Deciduous trees grow all over the world. They grow in parts of North America, Europe, and China. These places have four seasons in the year: spring, summer, autumn, and winter. In the autumn, the leaves of deciduous trees fall to the ground. But before they do, the leaves change color. They go from green to orange, brown, and red. Some people think autumn is the most beautiful season.

Oak trees and apple trees are deciduous. In the spring, they have small flowers. These flowers become fruit and seeds in the autumn. In the winter, the trees have no leaves. Then the leaves and flowers grow back again in the spring.

apple tree

Do you have a favorite kind of tree?

There are a lot of animals in the deciduous forest biome. They eat plants, fruit, and the seeds from the trees. Some of them hibernate. They sleep all winter when it's cold and there isn't much food.

Why are the animals that live in deciduous forests usually brown?

Words in Context

Find these words in the reading. What do you think they mean?

deciduous **hibernate** **coniferous** **survive** **adapt**

Coniferous Forests

Like deciduous trees, coniferous trees grow all over the world. Many of them grow in places that have longer and colder winters. This means that the summers are shorter and cooler, too.

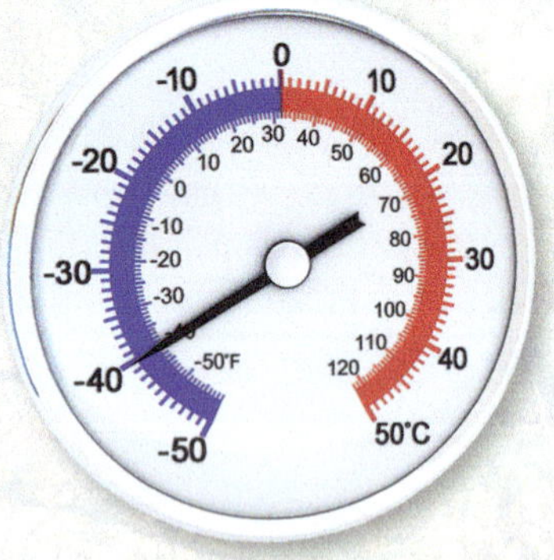

In some coniferous forests, the winter temperature can drop to –50°C!

We call these forests coniferous because the trees have cones instead of flowers or fruit. They also have thin, dark green leaves all year round. These leaves don't change color in autumn, so we call coniferous trees evergreen.

pine cone

Not many animals can survive in the very cold winters of the coniferous forests. Most of them hibernate. Many of them change color in the winter so they can hide in the snow. Some of them have thick white fur, not brown fur. This is one way they adapt.

The trees and animals in these two types of forests are very different, but they must all adapt to changes in their biomes to survive.

Why do animals in coniferous forests often have thick white fur or feathers in winter?

Explore the Reading

A Read and check (✔).

	Deciduous Forests	Coniferous Forests
1 The trees don't lose their leaves in autumn.	◯	✔
2 Winters are shorter here.	◯	◯
3 The animals find food in the trees.	◯	◯
4 The leaves stay the same color in autumn.	◯	◯
5 Some animals change color in winter.	◯	◯
6 The leaves of these trees are not thin.	◯	◯

B Read and match. How do trees and animals adapt to the cold?

1 
Deciduous Trees

3 
Bears

2 
Coniferous Trees

4 
Hares

a. have thin leaves.

b. lose their leaves in autumn and grow them again in spring.

c. change from brown to white.

d. hibernate and wake up in spring.

C Think and write. How do you adapt to your environment?

Spring	Summer

Autumn	Winter

A Think and check (✔). Why did the author write *The Beginning of Alice's Adventures*?

The author wrote *The Beginning of Alice's Adventures* to ...

- ◯ teach me about rabbits.
- ◯ help me understand Alice.
- ◯ help me have fun.

When we read, we should think about why the author wrote it. This is the **author's purpose**. Authors usually write to teach something, change someone's opinion, or entertain. Sometimes there is more than one purpose.

B Read and write *Yes* or *No*. Then write the author's purpose.

A New Friend

Every spring, a swallow comes back and builds her nest under the roof of Go Ne's house. This year, the swallow has two baby birds. One of them falls out of the nest. Go Ne and his father help it. How does the mother bird thank them? Who is Wen Shu and what does he do? Read and find out!

1 Does the author want to entertain me? ____________

2 Does the author want to teach me about birds? ____________

3 Does the author want me to change my opinion about birds? ____________

4 I think the author's purpose is to ______________________________.

C Think and discuss. Think about something you wrote. Why did you write it? What was your purpose?

I wrote a poem for ...

Now read A New Friend

Fiction

A New Friend

Every spring, a swallow built its nest under Go Ne's roof. Go Ne loved all animals, but the swallows were his favorite.

This spring, there were two baby swallows inside the nest.

Do you like spring? Why?

One day, one of the baby swallows fell out of the nest. Go Ne's father climbed up and put the baby bird back in its nest. The mommy bird was really happy and gave Go Ne a strange, gold seed. He planted it in a pot.

The plant grew bigger. It had a dark green stem and the most beautiful leaves.

Words in Context

Find these words in the reading. What do you think they mean?

swallow roof hit slingshot paid

After a few weeks, there was a big, round fruit. "Let's cut it open!" Go Ne's mom said. It was full of gold coins. They were rich!

Wen Shu saw the gold coins. He had an idea and ran to the nest.

"I want a seed, too!" he shouted. He pulled his slingshot back and let go. A stone sailed through the air. It hit the swallows' nest. It scared the baby birds and one fell.

slingshot

catapult

Why did Wen Shu do that?

Wen Shu ran to the little bird to put it back in the nest, but it didn't move. Go Ne heard Wen Shu and ran to help. He put the bird in his bike's basket and rode away.

Wen Shu followed Go Ne. He felt really sorry about the baby bird now. The two boys waited and waited.

After a long time, the vet came out with the baby swallow. It was OK!

Go Ne paid the vet with some of the money from the gold seed.
Go Ne, why did you spend that money? Now we don't have enough to fix the roof!
What do you do when you're sorry?
Later that day, Wen Shu went to Go Ne's house. He left a special gift so they could fix the roof. Go Ne and his family were very happy. And Wen Shu was, too.

Explore the Reading

A Read and answer.

1 What is Go Ne's favorite season?

Go Ne's favorite season is spring.

2 How did Go Ne's father put the baby swallow back in its nest?

3 What did Go Ne do with the gold seed?

4 What did Wen Shu want?

5 How did Wen Shu feel about what happened to the bird?

B Look and read. Then match the sentences to the characters.

1 He left things in the yard.

2 His family needed to fix their roof.

3 He always helped the birds.

4 He hurt the baby bird.

5 He took the baby bird to the vet.

6 He was sorry for what he did.

C Think and check (✔). What else did you learn from the story?

1 Be nice to some people. ◯

2 Be kind to animals and people. ◯

3 Friends are not important. ◯

Spelling Pattern *ai*

Listen and write. Then check your answers.

1 r_____ 2 m_____ 3 p_____ 4 t_____ 5 c_____

Now find more words spelled with *ai* in the reading.

How are plants, animals, and humans connected?

A Think and write. What do trees and plants give to people and animals?

B Imagine a world without trees or plants. What happens? Make a list together. Do a Roundtable.

C Think and discuss. What's on your list?

Without trees, birds can't ...

Without plants, people can't ...

My Reading Journal

Which places in this unit do you want to visit? What do you want to see?

I want to visit ______________________.

I want to see ______________________.

What is one thing you learned about plants or animals?

I learned ______________________.

UNIT 3

How Much Is It?

Think, Pair, Share

A Look at the picture. What labels do you want on your jars? Think about it.

B Discuss with your partner.

> Do you want a label for college?

> Of course I do!

C Share your ideas with the class.

> We both want labels for college.

D Where do people use money? Make a class list of places.

E Think and discuss. What's wrong? How can they fix it?

One farmer needs a goat. The other farmer needs some grain.

Now read The History of Money

Nonfiction

THE HISTORY OF MONEY

Thousands of years ago, people didn't use money. Instead, people bartered for things they wanted. Around 6000 BCE, if someone wanted to buy a new goat, he paid for it with grain. But it took time to agree how much things were worth.

Then, in 1200 BCE, people started using cowrie shells as money. The shells were easier to carry than goats or bags of grain.

BCE stands for Before Common Era. BCE dates count backwards, so something from 6000 BCE is older than something from 1200 BCE. Can you guess what CE stands for?

After that, around 1000 BCE, the Chinese started using metal money. At first, they used small metal knives and spades. But this money was difficult to carry and to use. Later, probably between 400 and 300 BCE, people started to use round metal money with holes in the middle.

Why do you think they put holes in the coins?

However, around 600 BCE, one of the kings of Lydia, which is part of modern-day Turkey, made the first true coins. These coins had pictures of plants and animals on them. Everyone knew how much each coin was worth.

Words in Context

Find these words in the reading. What do you think they mean?

bartered metal valuable credit card plastic

Soon, many countries made their own coins from valuable metals like silver and gold. This made buying and selling easier.

The first paper money came from China between 800 and 900 CE. It was easier to carry than metal coins. European countries didn't start to use paper money widely until around 1600 CE.

A **timeline** is an infographic that shows information in time order.

After that, money didn't change for many centuries. Then, in 1958, there was the first credit card. People didn't have to use paper money or coins. Instead, they could use a small plastic card.

Do you wish we used different money today?

Today, in the 21st century, many people use electronic money. Because it's very easy to move around, people often use it to buy things on the internet.

What type of money do you think is going to be next?

800–900 CE

First paper money

1958 CE

First credit card

A Think and check (✔). Which of these is or was money?

1 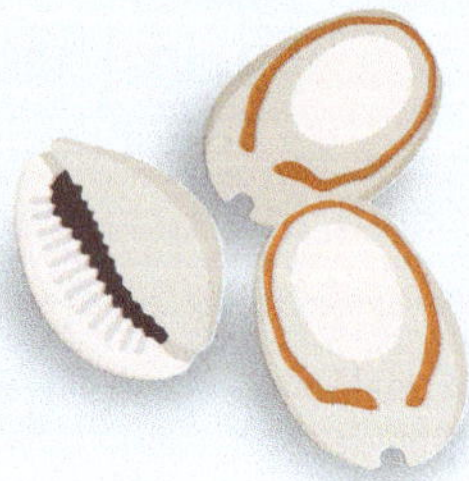
cowrie shells ◯

4 
wallet ◯

2 
fork and knife ◯

5 

paper money ◯

3 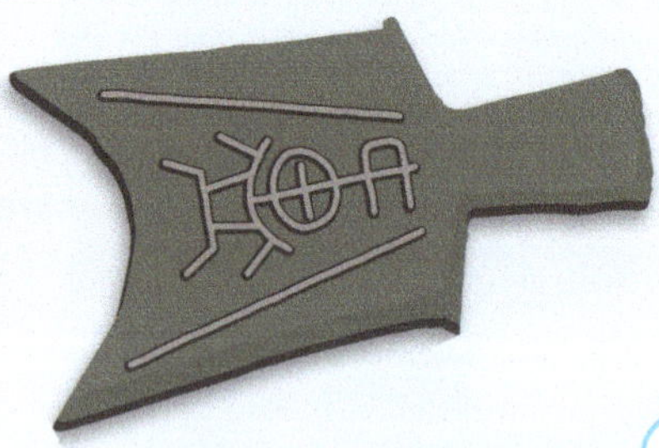
ancient Chinese knife ◯

6 

credit card ◯

B Compare and contrast the types of money. Complete the chart.

Type of Money	When It Was Used	What It Was Made From
	1200 BCE	
Knives and spades		
	800-900 CE	
		plastic

C Think and discuss. Design the next type of money.

I think the next type of money will be ...

A Read this retelling of *A New Friend*. Then write the problem and the solution.

One day, Go Ne and his father helped a baby bird. To say thank you, the mommy bird gave them a special seed. Wen Shu wanted one, too. But he used his slingshot. It was a mistake.

The baby bird was hurt! Go Ne and Wen Shu took it to the vet. They asked for help. The boys waited together. After a long time, the vet came out. The baby bird was OK, and Wen Shu learned about being a friend.

1 Problem: ______________________

2 Solution: ______________________

A **problem** is something difficult that happens in stories and in our lives. We can fix problems. A **solution** is a way to fix the problem. We can find many solutions.

B Think and write. Look at these pictures of early money. What were the problems with them? What solutions did people use?

1 

Problem: ______________________

Solution: ______________________

2 

Problem: ______________________

Solution: ______________________

C Think and discuss. Think of a problem you had. What did you do? How did you fix it?

One time, I ...

Now read **The $100 Bill**

Fiction

The $100 Bill

bill

note

"Hey, Paige, what's your phone number?" asked Nina after school. Paige shook her head.

"You know I don't have a cell phone."

"Oh, Paige! You really should get one!" Jodie laughed hard. Nina laughed too.

How do you think Paige feels?

Paige walked through the park on her way home. In her head, she could hear the girls laughing.

Then Paige saw something in the leaves.

Words in Context

Find these words in the reading. What do you think they mean?

belong to **return** **pocket** **restaurant** **money is tight**

What does Paige want to ask?

She picked it up. A hundred dollars! The bill was wet and dirty. Who did it belong to? There was no one to ask and no way to return it.

Paige didn't know what to do. Was it wrong to keep it? Suddenly, Jodie was next to her.

"What are you doing?" Jodie asked.

"Nothing," said Paige. She quickly put the money in her pocket.

"See you tomorrow, Paige!" said Jodie.

How do you think Paige feels about Jodie?

On the other side of the park, there was a cell phone store. Paige looked in the window. There was a beautiful black phone.

Paige touched the bill in her pocket. She could buy a cell phone now. *$95* ... she thought. *That's expensive, but ... no more laughing from Jodie and Nina!*

Did Paige do the right thing?

Paige went into the store.

"Can I help you?" the cashier asked. Paige touched the bill in her pocket again.

"Um, no, thank you," Paige answered. *I should save the money,* she thought.

Paige's dad sat in the kitchen. He looked really tired.

"Hi, honey," he said, and gave her a hug.

"Dad? I have an idea," said Paige. "Let's go out to a restaurant."

"Oh, Paige, I'd like to, but you know money is tight right now," he answered.

Paige smiled. "You don't have to pay, Dad!"

"Where did you find that?" he asked.

Paige told him about finding the money in the park.

"There's no way to give it back," her dad said. "OK. Let's go. I'm hungry!"

How does Paige feel at the end of the story?

Explore the Reading

A Write *True* or *False*. Say the page where you found the answer.

1 Jodie and Nina laughed at Paige because she didn't have a cell phone. ______

2 Paige found $10 in the park. ______

3 Paige put the bill in her pocket. ______

4 Paige bought a cell phone. ______

5 Paige and her dad wanted to have dinner together. ______

6 Paige and her dad ate pizza at the restaurant. ______

B Read and complete the story map.

Title: ______

Settings: ______

Main character: ______

Problem 1: ______

Solution: ______

Problem 2: ______

Solution: ______

C Think and discuss. Do you think Paige did the right thing by picking up the money? What would you do?

I think Paige ...

I would ...

Spelling Pattern *ar*

Listen and write. Then check your answers.

1 b______ 2 c______ 3 w______ 4 l______ 5 g______

Now find more words with *ar* in the reading.

Why do we need money?

A Look at the two readings. What are some of the different ways to use money? Think and discuss.

You can buy ...

You can go ...

B Think and discuss. Imagine you have these problems. What could you do? Do a Three-step Interview and complete the table.

Problem	Solution
You find $50.	
Your friend gives you a book as a present, but you already have the same book.	
Your mom gives you some money for video games and tells you to share it with your sister.	
You want a new toy, but you don't have enough money.	

C Think and share. Choose one problem from **B**. What should you do?

I should ...

My Reading Journal

The author wants new covers for the readings in this unit. Draw them.

Do you know any other stories where money is a problem?

UNIT 4

We Can Do It

Think, Pair, Share

A Look at the picture. How are they working together? Think about it.

B Discuss with your partner.

> The dancers are moving with the music.

> The musicians are playing it.

C Share your ideas with the class.

> We think everyone is listening to one another.

D Think and discuss. What is better when people work as a team?

E How does the team work together to get a basket? Put the events in order.

☐

☐

☐

Now read **Teamwork Makes the Dream Work**

Nonfiction

Teamwork Makes the Dream Work

WNBA is short for the Women's National Basketball Association. It's a professional women's basketball league in the United States that started in 1996. There are twelve teams in the WNBA. Some of the teams are the Minnesota Lynx, the Los Angeles Sparks, the Dallas Wings, and the New York Liberty. They play 34 games each season in front of huge crowds all over the country.

How do you score a point in basketball?

In a basketball game, ten players are on the court—five from each team. Each team has a basket at one end of the court. A player has to get the ball into the other team's basket to score points, but all the teammates have to work together to make this happen. Most baskets are worth two points, but from far away, they're worth three.

In one of the championship games, the Los Angeles Sparks were playing against the Minnesota Lynx. The game was almost over, and the Los Angeles Sparks were losing by five points. Chelsea Gray, a Sparks player, was in the air shooting the ball. And she scored a three-pointer! But three points weren't enough, and the Minnesota Lynx won the game. That didn't stop the Sparks, though. They worked even harder and won the championship that year!

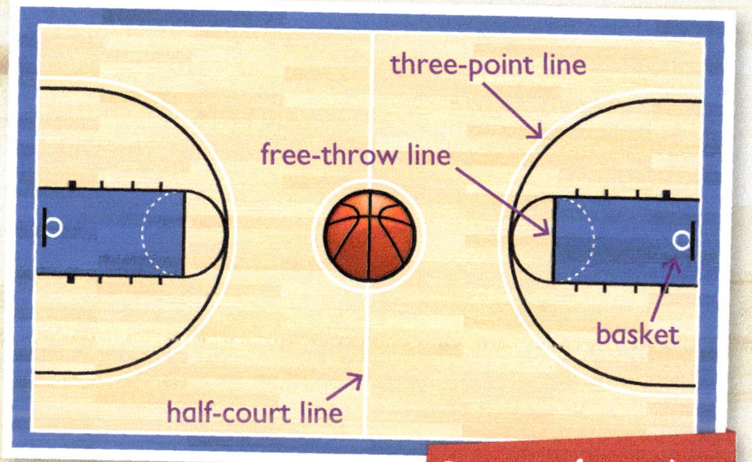

Do you prefer watching or playing sports?

Winning is important, but it isn't everything. Working together is part of playing the game. Some of the players from the Sparks and the Lynx talk about teamwork.

Chelsea Gray

"My team needed me."

Candace Parker

"My teammates and my coaches were always there for me."

Maya Moore

"No matter what we're feeling that day, we have to do our best ..."

Lindsay Whalen

"As a group we have to do it, but everybody has to bring it."

A **quote** is something someone said. Which is your favorite? Why?

These WNBA players know that teamwork makes their dream work. Their dream, of course, is to win the championship next year.

Words in Context

Find these words in the reading. What do you think they mean?

league court basket score shooting

Explore the Reading

A Write *True* or *False*. Say the page where you found the answer.

1 The WNBA began in 1996. ________

2 The WNBA started in the United Kingdom. ________

3 There are 34 teams in the WNBA. ________

4 Most baskets are worth two points. ________

5 Chelsea Gray scored the last three points for her team. ________

6 The Los Angeles Sparks won the game. ________

B Think and complete. What did you already know about basketball? What did you learn?

What I Knew

What I Learned

C Think and discuss. What sports teams are in your area? How do people in your city feel about them?

In my city ...

Spelling Pattern *or*

Listen and write. Then check your answers.

1 s________ 2 h________ 3 a________ 4 f________ 5 a________

Now find more words with *or* in the reading.

A Look at *Teamwork Makes the Dream Work* again. Put the events in order.

- [ ] Chelsea Gray scored three points.
- [ ] The Minnesota Lynx won the game.
- [ ] Chelsea Gray was in the air.
- [ ] The Los Angeles Sparks were losing by five points.

The **sequence of events** is the order things happen in a reading. Knowing the order things happen helps us understand how the events are connected. This helps us follow the story better.

B Put the events in order.

Paige woke up early in the morning to get ready for school.

She changed into her uniform and raincoat, and then she left for school.

First, she ate a bowl of cereal for breakfast.

Then, she brushed her teeth and washed her face.

C Think and write. Look at the beginning of *Late for the Show*. What's the first event? What do you think happens after that?

The first event is ____.

After that, I think ____.

Now read **Late for the Show**

Fiction

Late for the Show

Twelfth Night by William Shakespeare
Characters and actors:

Riya as VIOLA

Arush as SEBASTIAN

Harry as THE TREE

Lynn as NARRATOR

Mr. David Williams

Harry's mom

Harry's dad

Narrator: *It's Friday afternoon. It's the last rehearsal for the only performance of "Twelfth Night" at Woodlands School.*

Mr. Williams: And … the end. Well done, everyone! Now, remember, the show starts at 6 o'clock tomorrow night, so please be here at quarter past five. And please remember to bring your costumes!

Children: Yes, Mr. Williams.

Harry: How did I do?

Mr. Williams: Great! Don't be nervous, Harry. It's your first time on stage.

Words in Context

Find these words in the reading. What do you think they mean?

show **calm** **platform** **sank** **alive**

UNDERGROUND
The subway in London is called the Underground or the Tube.
HARRY
Harry's dad: OK, Harry, you and Mom take the Underground! I'll stay here.
Harry: *(putting on his tree costume)* What time is it, Mom?
Harry's mom: Quarter past five. We're a bit late, but don't worry …
How does Harry feel?
Narrator: *Ladies and gentlemen, there's a problem with the train. Please stay calm.*

Narrator: *Five minutes later, the train is still not moving.*
Harry: We're never going to get there!
Narrator: *Ladies and gentlemen, please get off the train and wait on the platform. We're fixing the problem.*
Harry: *(surprised)* Arush! You're here!
Lynn: Me too … and Riya!

Riya: Look. We're too late!

Harry: The show should be happening now, but we're not on stage!

Lynn: Wait a minute …

Lynn: Why don't we perform the show here, now?

Harry: Good idea!

Riya: We have our costumes and an audience!

Arush: Yes, let's do it!

Lynn: *(as Narrator)* Viola wakes up on a beach after a storm. She was traveling on a ship with her brother Sebastian, but the ship sank. Now, Viola is alone, and she can't find Sebastian.

Riya: *(as Viola)* Sebastian! Where are you? … Oh, I'm so frightened.

Harry's mom: That's my son. He's the tree! Isn't he great?

theater

theatre

Do you like to watch plays at the theater or on TV?

Riya: *(as Viola)* Sebastian! You're alive!
Arush: *(as Sebastian)* Viola! My sister!

Mr. Williams: Bravo! Fantastic! Well done!

Mr. Williams: Great teamwork! You were fantastic! I'm so proud of you.
Harry: That was our best performance!
Riya: Yes! We did it together.
Narrator: Ladies and gentlemen, thank you for waiting. We fixed the problem. Please get back on the train.
Harry: It's too late now!
Can you think of a time you were late for something?

Explore the Reading

A Complete the story map.

Characters

Who:

Setting

Where:

When:

Title

Problem

What happened on the way to the show?

Solution

What happened on the subway platform?

B Put the events in order. Then retell the story to a partner.

- ☐ The train has a problem.
- ☐ Arush, Riya, Lynn, and Harry perform the play *Twelfth Night*.
- ☐ Harry's car is stuck in traffic.
- ☐ Harry finds Arush, Riya, and Lynn on the platform.
- ☐ Harry and his friends practice.
- ☐ Harry and his mother get on the train.

C Think and discuss. How did the characters work together to put on a play? How do you work with your teammates?

Lynn asks ...

Mr. Williams helps ...

How does teamwork help us?

A Compare and contrast the Los Angeles Sparks with Harry and his friends. Complete the Venn diagram.

Los Angeles Sparks	Both	Harry and his friends

B Think and discuss. How do the people on these teams help each other? Do a Numbered Heads Together routine.

- soccer team
- acting club
- dance team
- music club

Soccer players help each other when ...

C Think and discuss. Talk about a time teamwork helped you. What happened?

I'm on a team and I ...

Last year, I did ...

My Reading Journal

Find four words in this unit that are interesting or new to you. Write.

1 ______ 2 ______ 3 ______ 4 ______

Color the stars to rate the unit. Then write a short review.

☆ ☆ ☆ ☆ ☆ ______________________________

____.

UNIT 5

Make Some Noise

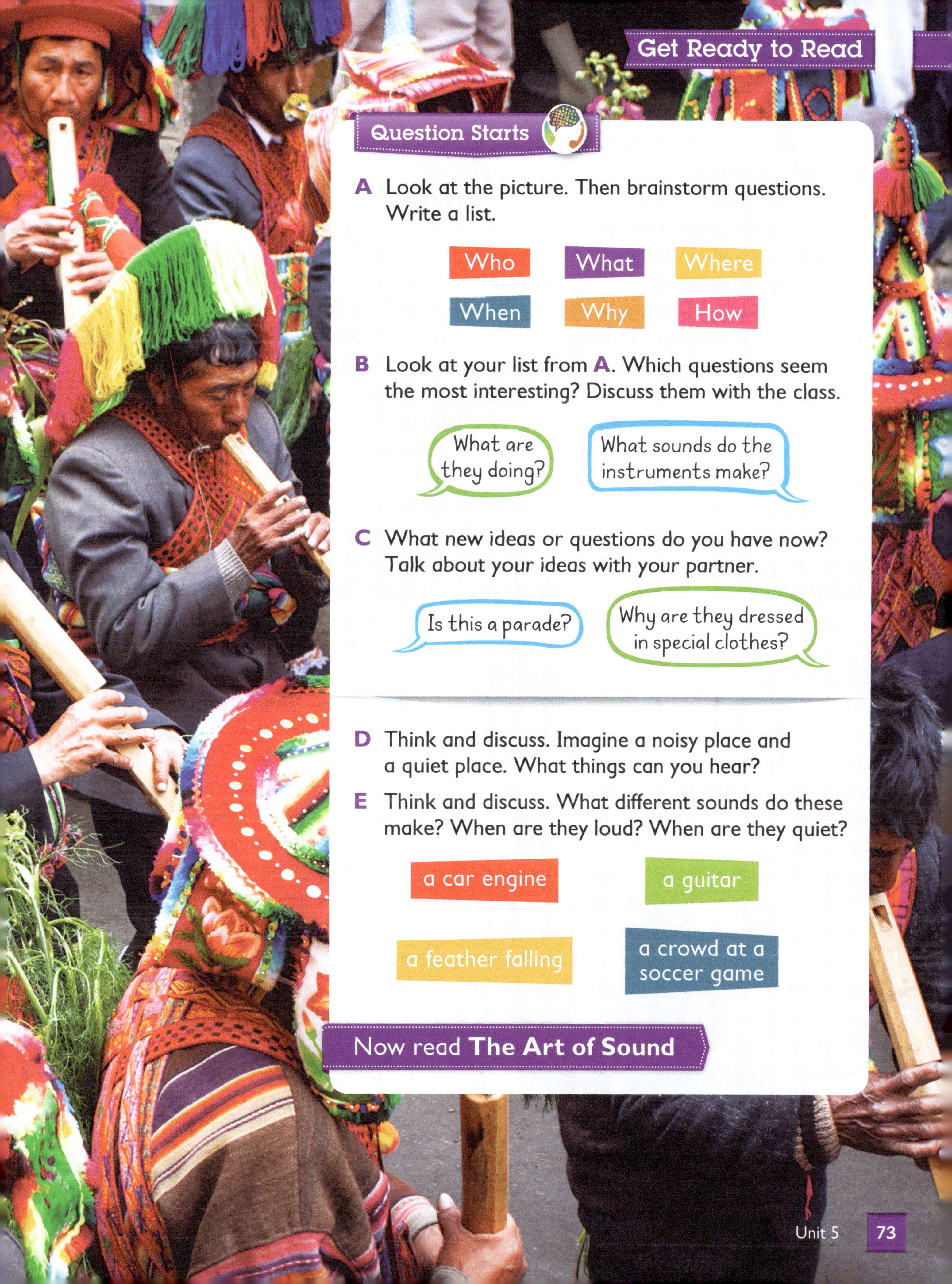

Question Starts

A Look at the picture. Then brainstorm questions. Write a list.

Who | What | Where
When | Why | How

B Look at your list from **A**. Which questions seem the most interesting? Discuss them with the class.

What are they doing?

What sounds do the instruments make?

C What new ideas or questions do you have now? Talk about your ideas with your partner.

Is this a parade?

Why are they dressed in special clothes?

D Think and discuss. Imagine a noisy place and a quiet place. What things can you hear?

E Think and discuss. What different sounds do these make? When are they loud? When are they quiet?

a car engine | a guitar
a feather falling | a crowd at a soccer game

Now read **The Art of Sound**

Nonfiction

THE ART OF SOUND

A knight runs through a castle, and a man chases after him. Their heavy boots thud on the floor. They pull out their swords. They fight. Their swords crash together with a loud smash.

Sound words like ***crash*** help us imagine what's happening.

But this isn't a real castle. It's fake. This is a movie. The swords are made of plastic. The castle is made of wood. So why are the sounds so realistic?

The name "Foley artist" comes from Jack Foley, one of the first people to work with sound in movies.

This is the job of a Foley artist, a person who puts special sounds into movies. A Foley artist is a sound artist.

Often when people make a movie, they only record the actors' voices. It is sometimes too noisy outside to record every sound, like a bee buzzing or a dog barking. But these sounds are important.

Foley artists record new sounds that are louder and clearer.

Words in Context

Find these words in the reading. What do you think they mean?

knight **swords** **realistic** **artist** **record** **voices** **studio**

Foley artists work in a special studio. They watch the movie and pay attention to what the actors are doing. When the actor walks on a wooden floor, the Foley artist makes the sound of footsteps. When the actor breaks a window, the Foley artist records the sound of real glass breaking. Is there going to be a storm in the movie? The Foley artist can make the sound of thunder by moving a thin piece of metal.

But are the footsteps going to be soft or loud? How much glass is going to break? How loud should the thunder be? Foley artists have to make everything sound realistic. They have to listen to how things sound in real life. Then they have to be creative to make new sounds.

What are different ways a Foley artist makes sounds?

Do you think it's fun being a Foley artist? Why or why not?

In a Foley studio, there are many tools. The artist uses different things to get the right sound.

There are different kinds of floors, shoes, and books. An old chair can make a loud squeak. Two pieces of coconut banged together can make the sound of a horse walking. Keys can make the sound of a knight marching. A head of lettuce can make a soft crunch. And a big book closing quickly can sound like a punch!

These are just a few of the sound artist's tricks.

Explore the Reading

A Answer the questions.

1 What does a Foley artist do?

2 Where does the name "Foley artist" come from?

3 Why do movies need a Foley artist?

4 Where does a Foley artist work?

5 What are some of the tools a Foley artist uses?

B Think and discuss. What makes a good Foley artist?

To be a good Foley artist, you need ...

Can you imagine what could make those sounds?

C Think and write. Imagine a Foley artist copied sounds from your day. What sounds would they make?

1 __________

2 __________

3 __________

4 __________

Spelling Pattern *ou*

Listen and write. Then check your answers.

1 t_____ 2 h_____ 3 c_____ 4 p_____ 5 y_____

Now find more words with *ou* in the reading.

A Draw and discuss. What can cause each of these sounds?

1 CRUNCH!   2 SQUEAK!   3 BUZZ!

In stories and in our lives, the reason something happens is the **cause**. The **effect** is what happens. We can see what changes. One cause can have many effects.

B Read these facts about Ludwig van Beethoven, a famous composer. Match the cause to the effect.

Cause

1 When he was young, he practiced his piano for many hours.

2 His family needed money.

3 He became friends with a famous teacher.

4 He lost his hearing.

Effect

a. He got a job.

b. He became a great piano player.

c. He couldn't hear music anymore.

d. He learned a lot about writing music.

C Think and discuss. Do all people hear well? Do you know anyone who doesn't hear very well or who can't hear?

My grandpa can't hear well, so he ...

Now read **Beethoven's 9th**

Fiction

Beethoven's 9th

The orchestra waits—violins, drums, and flutes.
Singers hum—women in dresses, men in suits.
They wait for Beethoven, the great composer.
The time for his music comes closer and closer.

Sensory details use your five senses to visualize a scene. Can you find some?

Beethoven's new music took him ten years,
At his piano, after lots of hard work and tears.
At last! He's on stage, his hair wild and gray,
There with the orchestra while they play.

Ludwig van Beethoven (1770–1827) was a famous composer from Germany.

Words in Context

Find these words in the reading. What do you think they mean?

composer eagle bends knees deaf

What words does the author use to help you see and hear more details?

The famous composer lifts his arms high,
And brings them down, like an eagle that flies.
The music floats through the air, soft and sweet,
Filling the room—front row to back seat.

Beethoven waves his arms here and there,
Light shines in his eyes, the wind's in his hair.
First, he stands tall, then bends down on his knees,
Like a small boat sailing on stormy seas.

Beethoven wrote the music, so he knows every note.
He stands proudly onstage, in his red scarf and coat.
Trumpets play loudly. Drums boom, voices cry,
The audience wonders how the time flies by.

At last it is finished, the crowd gets to their feet,
They clap and throw flowers. What a wonderful treat!
They shout Beethoven's name, their hands in the air,
But he cannot hear them. For him, they're not there.

Beethoven was probably around 25 when he started losing his hearing.

Then a kind singer turns him to look at the cheers,
The sad truth is, the composer can't hear.
Beethoven is deaf, his hearing long dead,
But the music is there, still alive in his head.

Why is Beethoven crying?
How would you feel?

Beethoven sees the people, and now it is clear.
His heart is happy, his eyes fill with tears.
They like his music, Beethoven feels proud.
He bends down low, thanking the crowd.

Beethoven can remember hearing well.
But now, his ears can no longer tell.
The musician is deaf, his hearing long dead,
But the music is there, still alive in his head.

Explore the Reading

A Read and choose.

1 What is the poem's setting?

(a.) a theater   b. a library   c. a sports center

2 Who is Beethoven?

a. a flute player   b. a composer   c. a singer

3 Which instruments go *boom*?

a. the drums   b. the flutes   c. the violins

4 What sounds does the audience make?

a. They talk to each other.   b. They hum and sing.   c. They clap, shout, and cheer.

5 Why does the singer turn Beethoven around?

a. So he can take a break.   b. So he can see the crowd cheering.   c. So they can hug.

B Think and check (✔). What effects did Beethoven's music have on the audience?

- ◯ They clapped and cheered.
- ◯ Time flew by for them.
- ◯ They fell asleep.
- ◯ It made them hungry.
- ◯ Everyone felt happy.

C Think, circle, and discuss. Do you ever listen to live music? Who do you listen with? How do those people feel? How do you feel?

happy   excited   alive   bored

sad   annoyed   frightened   angry

Sometimes, I listen to ...

I feel ...

What different types of sounds are in our world?

A Look at both readings. Find three different sound words. Write.

B Sit quietly. Close your eyes. What can you hear? Listen very carefully. Then complete the graphic organizer.

C Talk about the sounds you heard with your partner. Did any of them surprise you? Do a Think, Pair, Share.

I heard ...

My Reading Journal

Which is your favorite noise from the unit? Why?

I like the ______________ because ______________________________.

Look back at the unit. What questions do you have? What do you want to learn more about?

____

____

UNIT 6

That Looks Good

Activating Prior Knowledge About Cooking and Nutrition

See, Think, Wonder

A Look at the picture. What do you see?

I see a a smiley face!

I see chopsticks.

B What do you think?

I think it's a special lunch.

The food looks delicious!

C What do you wonder?

Is there a party?

How can I make food like this?

D Think and discuss. Do you like cooking? Why or why not?

E Look through *Little Chef* on the next page. What are the names of the characters? Write.

1 ____________________

2 ____________________

3 ____________________

Now read **Little Chef**

Fiction

Little Chef

Words in Context

Find these words in the reading. What do you think they mean?

delicious **frozen** **caramel** **winner** **advice**

We have only 20 minutes left, and everyone is working hard. Uh, oh! There's something wrong with Marisa's tower!
20:00

Oh, no! It's falling apart. I need to start again, but there isn't time. I don't know what to do. It's a disaster! Do I throw it out?
MARISA
FLOUR

What does *When life gives you lemons, make lemonade* mean?

Little Chef
Marisa, only 15 minutes left.
OK! I just need to add some more caramel and some salt.
15:00

... and time's up! Stop cooking everyone! Please carry your desserts to the table.
00:00

Well done! You all finished your desserts on time.
Now we have to decide which is the best. Marisa, what happened to your "Caramel Tower"?
Oh, I decided to change it. It's now called ... "Lemonade."
How interesting!
And the winner is ...
Marisa! Congratulations! You're our new "Little Chef"!
Your "Lemonade" was the most delicious and creative dessert. Where do you get your ideas?
Oh, I got some good advice from my grandpa.
Where do you get your ideas from?

Explore the Reading

A Read and choose.

1 The contestants have 20 / 40 / 60 minutes to make their dish.

2 Carlo's dessert has a lot of vanilla / chocolate / lemon juice.

3 Amy's dessert doesn't have mango / strawberries / pineapple.

4 Marisa's dessert is made of chocolate / ice cream / cookies.

5 Marisa won because her dessert was difficult to make / delicious / pretty.

B Draw. Look through *Little Chef* for details about the desserts. What did they look like?

1 Carlo's dessert

2 Amy's dessert

3 Marisa's dessert

C Complete the story mountain for *Little Chef*. Then compare and discuss.

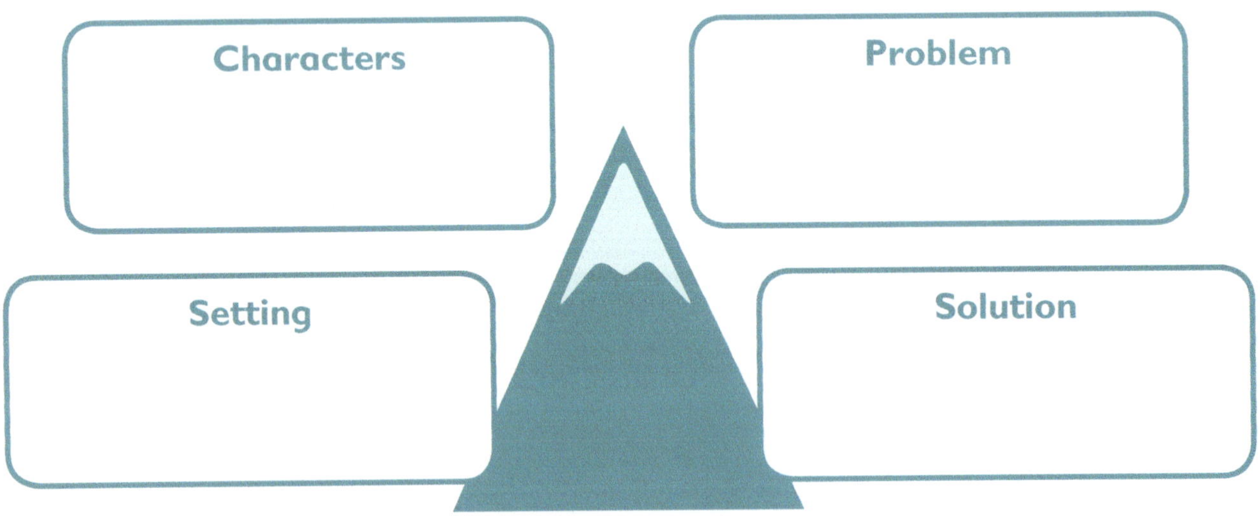

D Think and discuss. When Marisa had a problem, she thought about her grandpa. When you have a problem, who do you talk to?

I usually talk to ...

A Scan *Little Chef* and write the names of the desserts.

1 Carlo's dessert is called ____________________.

2 Amy's dessert is called ____________________.

3 Marisa's first dessert is called ____________________.

4 Marisa's winning dessert is called ____________________.

When we **scan** a text, we read quickly to find answers to questions. We look for the information without reading every word. When we find the information, we read that whole sentence to learn more.

B Read the questions. Scan the paragraphs for the answers and write.

1 The number of people this article is about: ____________________

2 Mikaila's age when she took part in the competition: ____________________

3 Mikaila was interested in: ____________________

4 Mikaila's last name: ____________________

Mikaila's Lemonade Story

Mikaila Ulmer was only four years old when she wanted to make a product for a children's business competition. But how did she decide what to make?

A few things helped Mikaila make a decision. First, she knew that she wanted to make something for Austin Lemonade Day. Then, a bee stung her twice. Mikaila didn't like the bee stings, but she became interested in bees and honey.

C Think and discuss. Imagine there is a children's business competition near you. What product would you make?

I'd make ...

Now read **Too Young to Cook?**

Nonfiction

TOO YOUNG TO COOK?

True Stories of Young Chefs

Mikaila Ulmer and Fraser Doherty love cooking. They both had great ideas that made them successful. Here are their stories:

Mikaila's Lemonade Story

Mikaila was only four years old when she wanted to make a product for a children's business competition. But how did she decide what to make?

A few things helped Mikaila make a decision. First, she knew that she wanted to make something for Austin Lemonade Day. Then, a bee stung her twice. Mikaila didn't like the bee stings, but she became interested in bees and honey.

Austin is in Texas, USA.

Then, Mikaila's great granny Helen sent her family a cookbook that included an old, special recipe for flaxseed lemonade.

Mikaila decided to make a product that helped the honeybees and used her great granny Helen's recipe. She came up with Me & the Bees Lemonade: a cold drink made from lemons, flaxseed, and local honey.

Today, Mikaila has a big company. She sells her lemonade and gives money to organizations that help honeybees. In 2016, she made an $11 million deal to sell Me & the Bees Lemonade in 55 stores across the USA.

Why are bees important to the environment?

Words in Context

Find these words in the reading. What do you think they mean?

successful flaxseed cookbook
experimented discovered elderly

Fraser's Jam Story

One afternoon when Fraser Doherty was 14, his grandmother taught him how to make jam.

Fraser began to make jam in the evenings and on weekends. He sold his jam in his hometown, Edinburgh. Then he experimented with his grandmother's recipe, trying many different ways to make the jam. In 2006, he discovered a way to make jam with fruit but no extra sugar.

Edinburgh is in Scotland, UK.

Fraser called his jam "SuperJam." He worked hard to design an interesting logo and found a factory to make his jam. In 2009, a large grocery chain agreed to sell his jam in their stores.

In 2010, Fraser wrote *The SuperJam Cookbook*. He also started organizing free "SuperJam Tea Parties" for elderly people, like his grandmother, who live alone. They dance, have tea, and of course, eat SuperJam! Today, people can buy SuperJam in stores all over the world.

How often do you cook with your family?

The kitchen is a fun place! Maybe one day, you can start a business just like Mikaila and Fraser.

Explore the Reading

A Read and complete.

sugar honeybees ~~bee stings~~ parties cookbook recipe

1 Mikaila didn't like the bee stings, but she still wanted to help the bees.

2 Mikaila used her great granny's ______________ to make lemonade.

3 Fraser shared his jam recipes in a ______________.

4 Mikaila wants to help save the ______________ because they're important.

5 Fraser's jam is different from his grandmother's because it has no ______________.

6 Fraser's ______________ make elderly people happier.

B Think and write. What did Mikaila and Fraser learn from their grandmothers? Who do you learn from in your family?

1 Mikaila learned ______________ ______________ from her grandmother.

2 Fraser learned ______________ ______________ from his grandmother.

3 I learned ______________ ______________ from my ______________.

C Think and discuss. Did you ever cook using a recipe? What did you make? How did it taste?

Last month, I used a recipe to make ...

I made ...

Spelling Pattern –*old*

Listen and write. Then check your answers.

1 g______ 2 c______ 3 t______ 4 h______ 5 f______

Now find more words ending with *old* in the reading.

Why is food important?

A Read and check (✔). What's true about the people from the readings?

	Marisa	Mikaila	Fraser
1 Cooking makes me rich.	◯	◯	◯
2 I learned how to cook when I was young.	◯	◯	◯
3 I learned to cook from my grandparents.	◯	◯	◯
4 I like to help others.	◯	◯	◯

B Think and write. Why is food important? Make a list.

- ______________________
- ______________________
- ______________________

C Think and discuss. What's your family's favorite recipe? What are the ingredients? Do a Three-step Interview.

My family's favorite recipe is ...

The ingredients are ...

My Reading Journal

Write three interesting things from this unit.

1 ______________________

2 ______________________

3 ______________________

What recipe do you want to make at home?

I want to make ______________________.

UNIT 7

How Can We Help?

See, Think, Wonder

A Look at the picture. What do you see?

I see a helicopter.

I see four people.

B What do you think?

I think the man is hurt.

I think they can help him.

C What do you wonder?

I wonder how fast the helicopter goes.

Are they doctors?

D What types of natural disasters do you know about? Brainstorm with a group.

I know about ...

They happen when ...

E Think and discuss. Look at the pictures on the first page of the reading. What do you think it's about?

I think it's about ...

Now read **What Happens Next?**

Fiction
What Happens Next?
What do you think *brought books to life* means?
It was story time. Everyone in our class loved story time.
Mr. Carlson, who is our favorite teacher, always brought books to life.

Just then, my desk started to shake. But it wasn't only my desk. It was my chair, too.

The shaking was gentle at first, but it got bigger and stronger.

Then, the whole classroom started moving from side to side. Pencils rolled off desks. Books fell off shelves.

Words in Context

Find these words in the reading. What do you think they mean?

gentle **crawl** **hot-air balloon** **rope** **loudspeaker**

What should you do in an earthquake?

Of course, we remembered what to do in an earthquake. We often practiced: stay calm, get on the ground, and crawl under something strong.

This kind of story is called **realistic fiction**. It's made up, but it could happen.

Soon, we were all under our desks. Everyone was scared. I looked at my twin sister Aiko, who was holding onto the legs of her desk. I smiled to help her feel less scared.

Then, Mr. Carlson did a strange thing. From under his desk, he started reading again.
Sophie climbed into the hot-air balloon and cut the rope that was keeping it tied to the ground. The balloon flew high into the air. She looked down at the city below ...
I closed my eyes and listened to Mr. Carlson.
I was in the hot-air balloon—flying through the sky. I could feel the wind on my face. I could see some birds that were flying near me. I was lost in the story.
How can you use your imagination to stay calm?

Then we heard the principal's voice on the loudspeaker.

Suddenly, I was back in our classroom. I looked around. Everything was still. The classroom wasn't shaking anymore.

principal

head teacher

We climbed out from under our desks. Everyone was still scared. Aiko smiled at me.

"But what happens next in the story, Mr. Carlson?" I asked. The class laughed. Mr. Carlson laughed, too.

Explore the Reading

A Put these events from the story in order. Then retell the story to a partner.

- [ ] The classroom wasn't shaking anymore.
- [ ] Soon, we were all under our desks.
- [ ] Then, Mr. Carlson did a strange thing. From under his desk, he started reading again.
- [ ] The whole classroom started moving from side to side. Pencils rolled off desks. Books fell off shelves.
- [ ] "But what happens next in the story?" I asked. The class laughed.

B Think and complete the graphic organizer. How did the class stay calm? Use details from the story.

How the Class Stayed Calm

C Write and discuss. When an emergency happens, what can you do to stay calm?

A Look at the title and picture below. Write what the reading is about. Then read and write why the reading is useful.

This reading is about ______________________________.

Tsunamis

Tsunamis are huge waves caused by underwater earthquakes. They can be very dangerous. To prepare for a tsunami, first find out about your town's plans for natural disasters. Is there a safe place to go? Make a plan for the best way to get there. Always keep a bag packed with things you will need, like food, water, and warm clothes.

This reading is useful because ______________________________.

Using what we know about a reading helps us make stronger conclusions. We make **predictions** *before* we read. We use the pictures and titles to make guesses.

We make **inferences** *after* we read. We read all the words and look at the pictures. Then we think about the reading and make more guesses.

B Think and write. Look at *Animals to the Rescue*. Predict what the reading is about.

I think it's about ______________________________

C Scan *Animals to the Rescue*. Write two animals that work. Predict their jobs.

Animal	Its Job

Now read **Animals to the Rescue**

Nonfiction

ANIMALS TO THE RESCUE

After a natural disaster, rescue workers have to work very quickly to find people who are hurt. They need to save people's lives. But when a building falls down, how do the rescue workers find the people who are trapped underneath? One solution is to use special search and rescue dogs.

People who train search and rescue dogs are called dog handlers. They train the dogs for 2 to 3 years. Dogs can smell very well. They can use their noses to find things, other animals, and people.

Some scientists think a dog's sense of smell is 10,000 times stronger than a human's!

Dogs can fit into very small spaces, so they can search in rubble more easily than people can.

The handlers take the dogs to the disaster zone and watch carefully to see where they go. The dogs really like finding people.

Why do people sometimes need animals in a natural disaster?

In April 2015, there was a huge earthquake in Nepal. Many people died. Search and rescue dogs worked hard to find survivors. Five days after the earthquake, dogs helped to find a 15-year-old boy who was trapped under a building and couldn't get out. He was still alive!

Words in Context

Find these words in the reading. What do you think they mean?

search train rubble survivors trapped safety stuck

Dogs aren't the only animals that help humans in an emergency.

Sometimes, after a big emergency, cars and trucks can't reach the disaster area. One solution is to use search and rescue horses.

Horses' ears can turn to hear noises better.

Horses can travel a long way over difficult ground. They can see well, and they can hear and smell better than humans. The rescue workers watch their horses carefully. Sometimes, the horses find survivors before the people do.

truck

lorry

Horses can also carry radios and other useful things. When the rescue workers arrive, they can help survivors and bring them to safety.

Wild animals can be heroes, too.

In 2009, a swimmer in China was stuck underwater. She couldn't move her legs, and she had no air. A whale pushed her up and saved her life.

In 2004 in New Zealand, some dolphins swam around a group of swimmers and saved them from a shark.

In an emergency, sometimes animals can help. They can even save lives.

Do you think dolphins and whales make good rescue animals?

Explore the Reading

A Think and check (✔). Why are these animals good for search and rescue?

1 Dogs are good for search and rescue because …

a. they have a strong sense of smell. ◯
b. they like going for walks. ◯
c. they can fit into small spaces. ◯
d. people can train them. ◯
e. they make good pets. ◯

2 Horses are good for search and rescue because …

a. they have tails. ◯
b. they can hear well. ◯
c. they can carry useful things. ◯
d. they can travel a long way. ◯
e. they like eating grass. ◯

B Think and discuss. Look back at your predictions on page 113. Were they correct?

Yes, I was right because ...

No, my prediction was ...

C Think, write, and discuss. How do you think the author feels about animals? Make an inference and give an example from the reading.

I think ____________ because the author said ______________________________.

D Choose and write. Do you think being a rescue worker is hard work? Why or why not?

I think it is / isn't hard work because ______________________________

____.

Spelling Pattern –ly

Listen and write. Then check your answers.

1 f________ 2 f________ 3 q________ 4 e________ 5 h________

Now find more words ending with *ly* in the reading.

How can we help each other in an emergency?

A Think and discuss. Look at both readings. How do people or animals work together in an emergency?

Mr. Carlson and his class ...

Dogs and people ...

B Think about natural disasters. How can you help? Complete the graphic organizer with a partner.

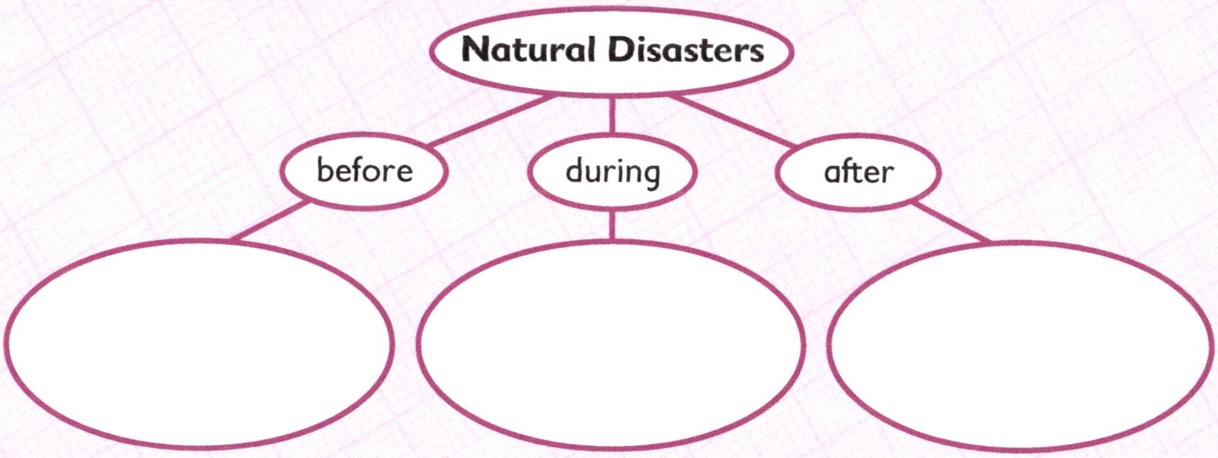

C Look at the graphic organizer in **B**. Do a Rally Robin.

We think you should ...

You can ...

My Reading Journal

Look back at the unit. Which part did you find the most interesting? What did you learn?

The most interesting part was ______________________________

______________________________.

I learned ______________________________

______________________________.

Now look back at the activities. How did you do? Color one face. Then write why.

____

____

UNIT 8 Under the Sea

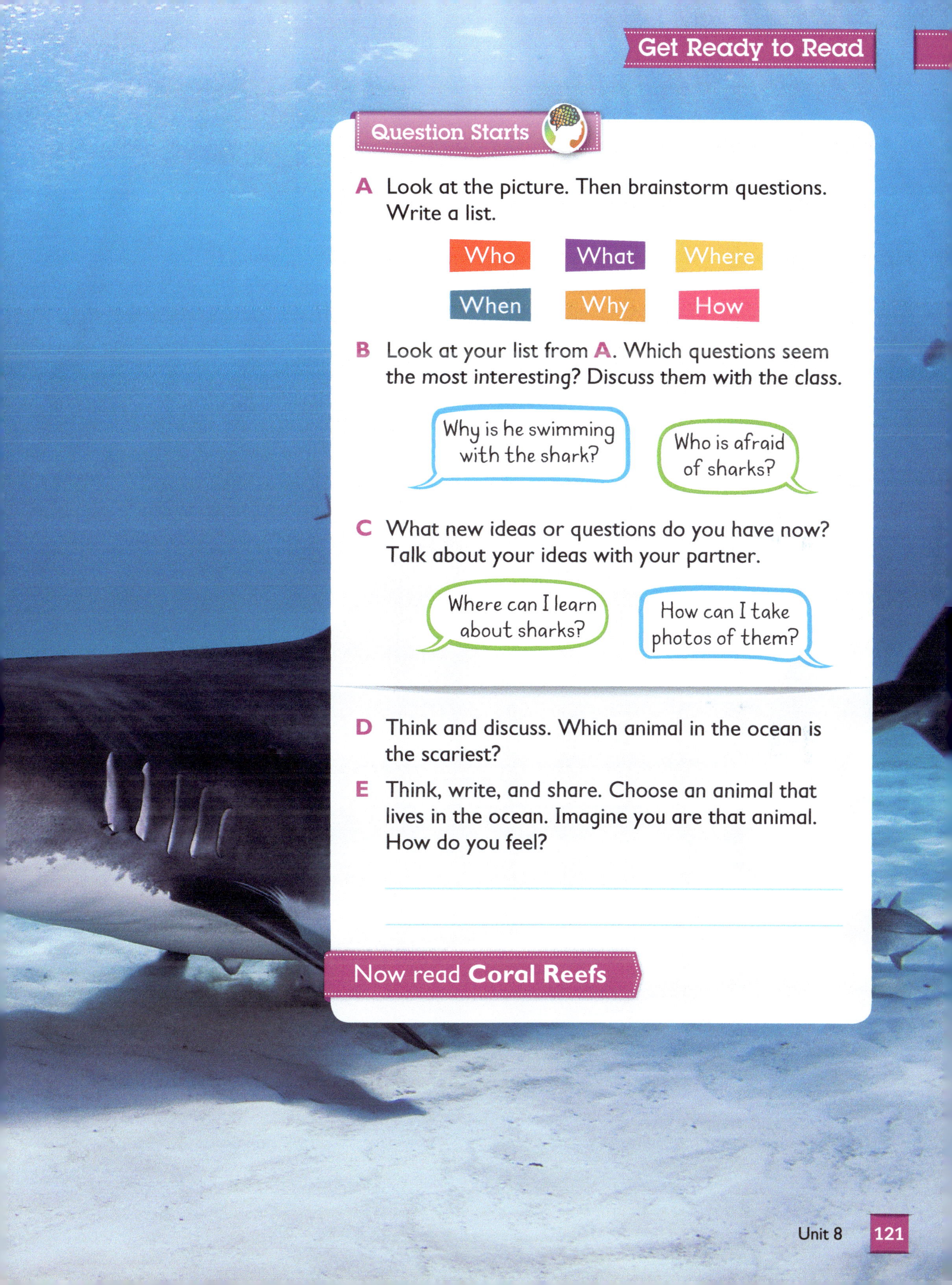

Question Starts

A Look at the picture. Then brainstorm questions. Write a list.

Who What Where

When Why How

B Look at your list from **A**. Which questions seem the most interesting? Discuss them with the class.

Why is he swimming with the shark?

Who is afraid of sharks?

C What new ideas or questions do you have now? Talk about your ideas with your partner.

Where can I learn about sharks?

How can I take photos of them?

D Think and discuss. Which animal in the ocean is the scariest?

E Think, write, and share. Choose an animal that lives in the ocean. Imagine you are that animal. How do you feel?

Now read **Coral Reefs**

Nonfiction

Coral Reefs

A World of Tiny Animals

There are fish, sharks, and whales in the world's oceans, but did you know there are also animals that look like mushrooms, trees, brains, and fingers? These are all coral!

There are two types of coral: soft and hard. Both are made of tiny animals called polyps.

Polyps are like jellyfish, but they don't swim. They stick to rocks, and after hundreds of years, they grow together and make a coral reef.

Coral get their bright colors from algae, very small plants that live inside the polyps. Algae need sunlight to grow, so they can only live in shallow water.

Coral polyps up close

Look for **captions** under pictures. What information do they give you?

Reefs as Shelter

Fish and other creatures such as sea turtles, starfish, and urchins need coral for food and shelter. The coral reefs protect small fish. The reef is their home. Some fish find food there when they are young, but leave the reef when they're old enough to swim away.

About two million species live in, on, and around coral reefs. That's 25 percent of all sea creatures!

Are Coral Reefs in Danger?

Today, all around the world, coral reefs are in danger. Here are three of the reasons:

- The sea is getting warmer. For coral to be healthy, the seawater can't be too cold or too hot. When the water is hotter than 28°C, the algae leave the reefs. This is why the coral are losing their color. When coral become white, they can die.
- The waste from big cities, including dangerous chemicals, often goes into the sea. Then the seawater becomes dirty and the coral don't get the sunlight they need.
- People who visit the reefs can touch the coral and damage them.

White, or bleached, corals

Protecting Coral Reefs

In many parts of the world, however, people take good care of coral reefs. In the city of Abu Dhabi, people protect the nearby Ras Ghanada reef. In Cuba, the coral reefs in "The Gardens of the Queen" are in a marine park. This means that no one can go fishing there and very few tourists can visit. Without protection like this, the coral reefs will die.

What can people do to protect coral reefs?

Words in Context

Find these words in the reading. What do you think they mean?

stick shallow creatures waste damage marine park

Explore the Reading

A Write *True* or *False*. Write the page where you found the answer.

1 Polyps are tiny animals that look like jellyfish. True 122

2 One polyp can grow into a coral. ______ ______

3 A coral reef is a large group of corals. ______ ______

4 Half of all the species in the sea can be found in or on coral reefs. ______ ______

5 Corals can't grow in water that's too cold or too hot. ______ ______

B Find the headings in *Coral Reefs*. Write. Then match to the main idea.

1 A World of Tiny Animals

2 ______

3 ______

4 ______

a. Coral reefs are in danger because of people.

b. Coral are made of tiny animals called polyps.

c. In many parts of the world, the reefs are protected.

d. Fish and other creatures use coral for shelter.

C Read and complete. Why are coral reefs in danger?

there isn't enough sunlight | they can damage them | the algae leave

1 When the seawater becomes too warm, ______.

2 When the seawater is dirty, ______.

3 When people touch the corals, ______.

D Think and discuss. Why is it important to protect coral reefs?

It's important because ...

Spelling Pattern –*ight*

Listen and write. Then check your answers.

1 n______ 2 r______ 3 t______ 4 f______ 5 l______

Now find more words ending with *ight* in the reading.

A Think and discuss. Look back at *What Happens Next?* on page 106. Who's telling the story about the earthquake? Imagine Mr. Carlson tells the story. How does the story change?

> Mr. Carlson would ...

Each character in a story has a unique **perspective**. They might tell a different story depending on how they feel about the events. When you read a story, think about the different characters' opinions about the same thing.

B Scan *The Lost Camera*. Which characters speak? Check (✔).

Sandy

Fin

Dr. Crab

Dollie

C Read and write. Who's telling the story?

My sister and I got ready for school that morning, like we do every day. I waited for her by the door. She looked for her backpack.

"Hurry up, Sandy. We can't miss the bus," I said.

"I'm coming, Fin!" she said to me. She put on her backpack and swam to the door. "Let's go!"

We hurried to the bus stop. The next thing we knew, we were on an adventure.

______________________ is telling the story.

Now read The Lost Camera

Fiction

The Lost Camera

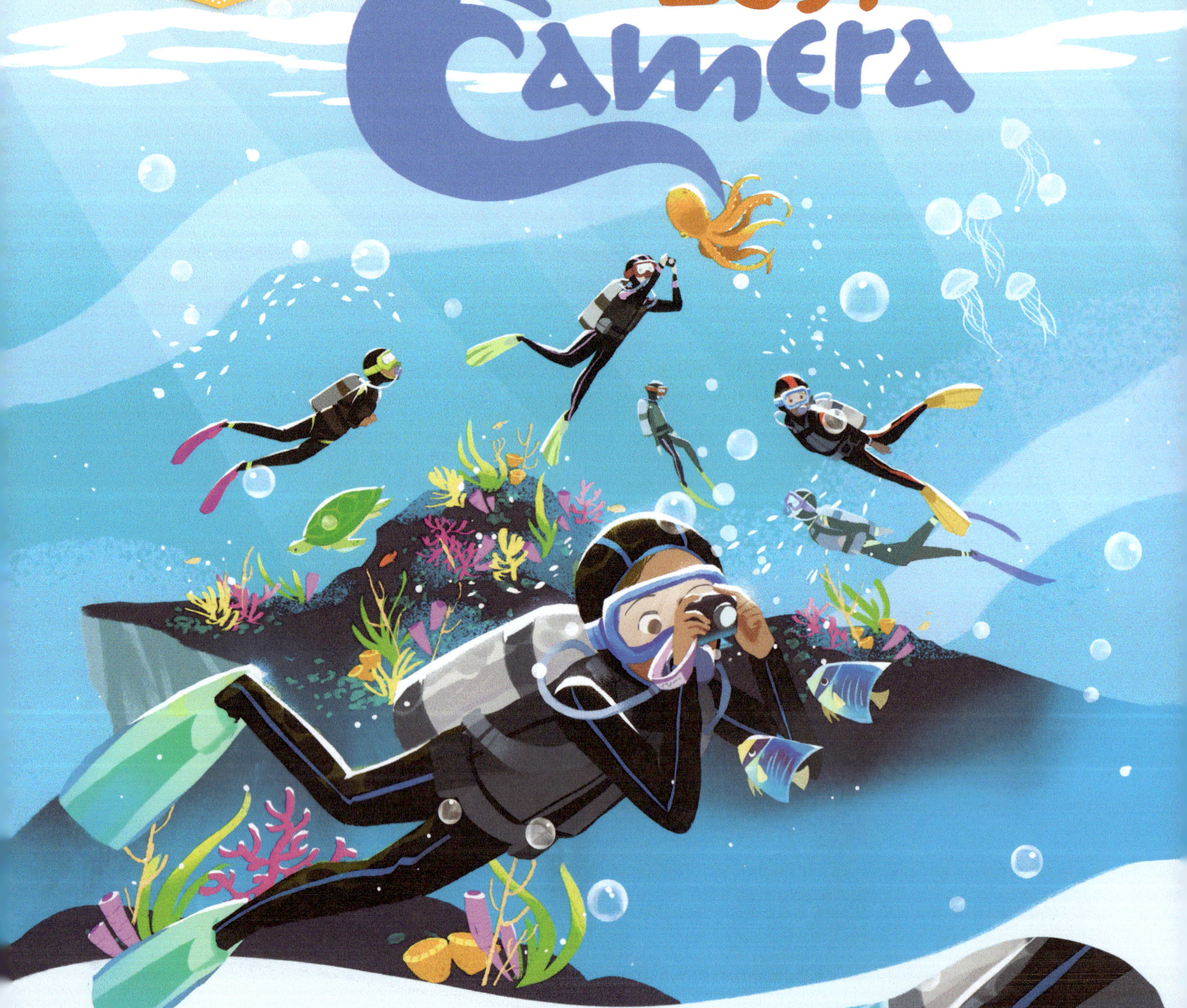

It was a normal day under the sea. Mom and Dad were going to work. My sister and I were swimming to school. Everyone was in a hurry.

Everyone … except the divers up near the surface. One of them needed a better photo of an angelfish. *Click!*

But suddenly the camera slipped out of her hand. It fell down, down into the dark water of the ocean … and into our world!

Do you think the diver will get her camera back?

How do the creatures in Seaville travel around?

Thud! The camera landed on the ocean floor, but nobody saw or noticed it …

Words in Context

Find these words in the reading. What do you think they mean?

divers surface slipped noticed tag everywhere

… except Sandy and me.

“Where did this come from?” Sandy asked.

I pointed up. “From divers up there.”

I looked at the tag on the camera closely. “Where’s Mexico?” I asked.

"There! I told you Mexico was real," Sandy whispered.

"I'd like to see this world," I told Sandy.

Then she had an idea. "Let's take the camera back to Mexico!"

"But how can we get there?" I asked.

"Dollie! Take us to the surface, please!" I shouted.

Dollie swam and swam. Up and up we went.

"Say *starfish*!"

The surface was so exciting. It was our first time there.

Suddenly, we saw something. It was a boat. There were people on it. Divers!

"Quick, Fin! Let's swim to the boat!" Sandy shouted.

Thump! The camera landed on the boat.

"Did you hear something?" one diver asked.

"Hey, my camera!" said another diver. "I was looking everywhere for that."

Can you answer Sandy's question?

Sandy and I wanted to see some more. Mexico was amazing!

"Wow! Those buildings are so tall!" I said.

"What are the children making?" Sandy asked. I didn't know, but it looked cool!

We were having a great time until …

Why are they feeling sick?

"I'm feeling sick," Sandy said.

"Me too," I said.

We were on the surface for too long, and breathed too much air.

"Quick, Dollie! Take us home. Sandy is sick," I shouted.

"Fin, what's wrong with your sister?" Dad asked me. I didn't want to tell him. I thought he would be angry with us.

"You're airsick, Sandy. Just rest a little and you'll be fine," Dr. Crab said.

"Airsick? Where did you go?" Dad asked.

"Tell us what happened, Fin—EVERYTHING!" Mom said.

"It's a long story, Mom," I said.

Explore the Reading

A Read and choose.

1 No one sees the camera except Fin and Sandy because …

a. they're too busy.   b. it's too small.   c. it's too dark.

2 Fin and Sandy are interested in the camera because …

a. it's better than their camera.   b. they like taking photos.   c. it's from a strange world.

3 Fin and Sandy bring the camera back because …

a. they want to see Mexico.   b. they don't want it anymore.   c. they want to talk to people.

4 Fin and Sandy don't feel well on the surface because …

a. they need air.   b. air isn't good for them.   c. they need food.

5 To feel better, Sandy has to …

a. drink juice.   b. have soup.   c. stay in bed.

B Read and match. Imagine there's another scene of *The Lost Camera*. Who says each sentence?

1 "Don't be angry at Fin. I wanted to go up to the surface, too."   Mom

2 "Sandy wasn't very sick, but they should never go to the surface."   Fin

3 "I was really enjoying myself until Sandy got sick."   Sandy

4 "I can't believe they swam to the surface. It's so dangerous!"   Dr. Crab

C Think and discuss. How would the story be different from Sandy's perspective?

D Think, write, and discuss. Choose a character. How does he or she feel at the beginning, middle, and end of the story?

My character:
Beginning:
Middle:
End:

What is life like under the sea?

A Think, discuss, and write. Look at the pictures in the unit. Complete the graphic organizer about what lives under the sea.

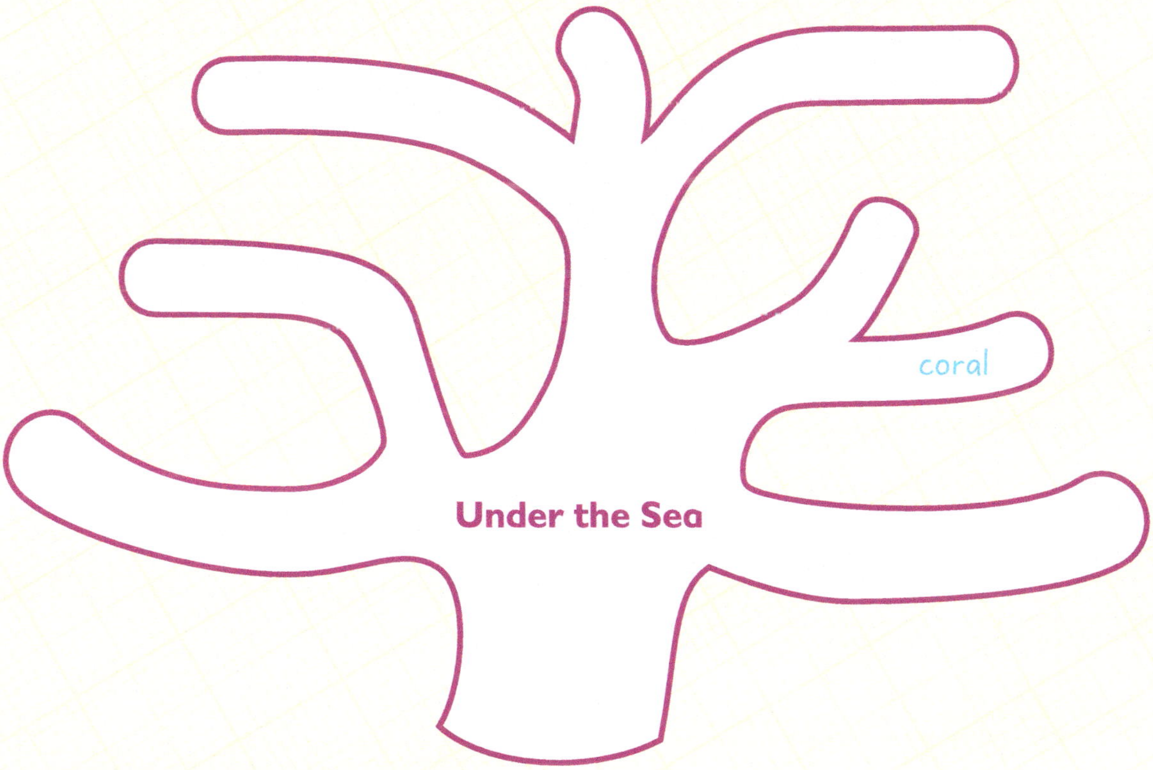

B Think and discuss. How is life under the sea different from life on land or in the air? Do an Inside-Outside Circle.

Under the sea there's ...

Animals can ...

My Reading Journal

Which setting from this unit would you like to visit—a coral reef or Seaville?

I'd like to visit ______________ because ______________.

How can we help protect sea life? Make a list.

______________ ______________

______________ ______________

UNIT 9

What's the Matter?

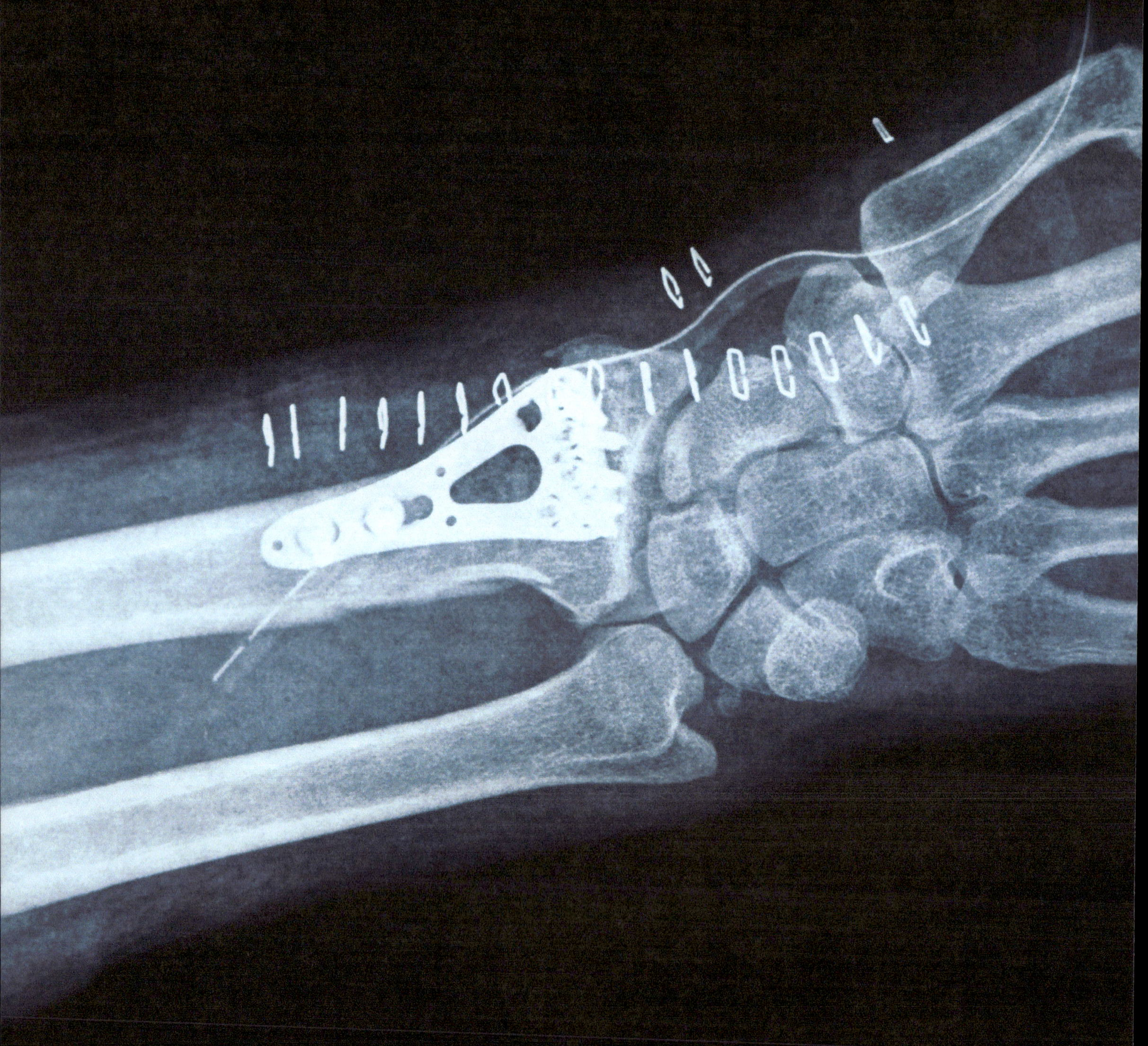

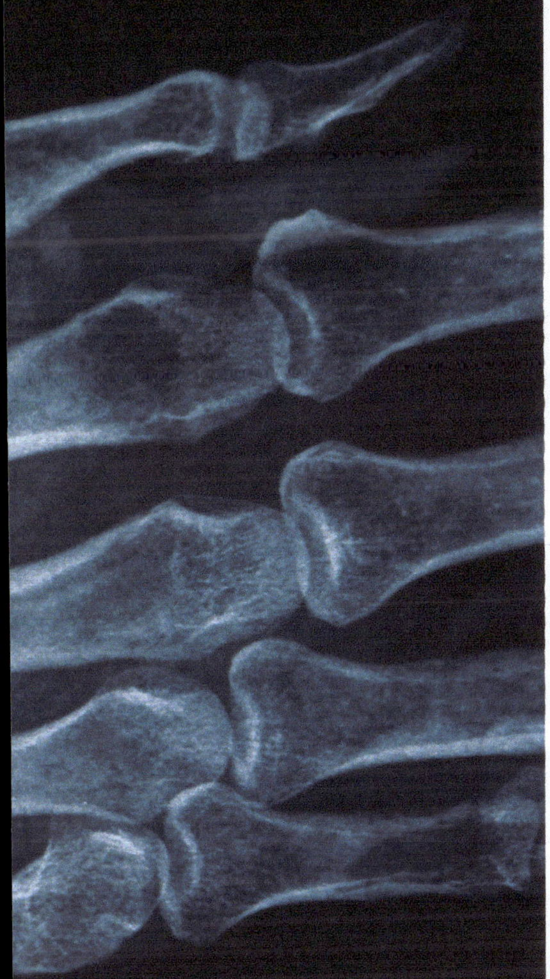

Think, Pair, Share

A Look at the picture. Imagine you're the doctor. What's the matter? Think about it.

B Discuss with your partner.

What do you think?

I think there's a broken bone.

C Share your ideas with the class.

We think it's getting better.

D Think about a time when you were sick. What was wrong? What made you well?

E Think, write, and discuss. Look at the next page. What is the reading about? What are two interesting details you can see?

1 It's about ______________________________
______________________________.

2 I see ______________________________
and ______________________________.

Now read **Take Your Medicine**

Nonfiction

Take Your Medicine

Most of us don't like being sick. Visiting the doctor's office, taking medicine, getting shots, and staying in bed—it isn't fun, is it?

But you should be happy you aren't living in the past, when doctors had some very different ideas about how to cure sick people.

Let's take a trip into the past and look at some old treatments.

shot
sick

injection
unwell

3300 BCE

For cuts and scrapes, people didn't use a bandage made of cloth or plastic. Sometimes, they used moss.

2500–2000 BCE
Ancient Egypt

A patient with sore bumps on his neck got interesting medicine made from the blood of birds and flies.

For toothaches, the ancient Egyptians took medicine made from dead mice.

2000 BCE
Ancient Mesopotamia

Do you grind your teeth while sleeping? The ancient Babylonians had a cure: Sleep with a human skull next to you for a week and you'll stop biting down on your teeth while you sleep.

Words in Context

Find these words in the reading. What do you think they mean?

cure treatments patient grind opposites disease

800–100 BCE
Ancient Greece

Do you feel some pain? In ancient Greece, healers put big, wet sponges on the places that hurt.

20 BCE–400 CE
Ancient Rome

The ancient Romans thought that opposites were good treatments. If a patient had a fever, a healer put cool cucumbers on the patient's body. If a patient felt cold, a healer told the patient to eat hot peppers.

have a fever (US)
have a temperature (UK)

What other opposites can you think of?

200–300 CE
China

To stay healthy and live forever, the treatment was to eat or drink some gold.

1300s Europe

There were many strange treatments for the plague, a terrible disease which killed millions of people. Sick people sometimes wore dead toads around their necks, or put chicken feathers on their sores. They thought this made the plague leave their bodies.

1800s Britain

For a sore throat, the treatment started on the feet. The sick person put a really dirty sock around their neck!

The patient tied a cooked potato to their head to cure an earache.

And doctors used leeches for all sorts of problems.

A leech is a little like a worm but it sucks blood.

Dirty socks and dead mice?
Bird blood and leeches? Yuck!
Aren't you glad you see a nice,
friendly doctor when you're sick?

Why do you think people in the past had such different ideas about medicine?

A Complete the table.

Sickness	Treatment	Where & When
1 a toothache		
2 a fever		
3 a sore throat		
4 an earache		
5 the plague		

B Think and discuss. Do you think any of those treatments cured people? Why or why not?

No, I don't think so because ...

C Write and discuss. What happens when you go to the doctor? Make a list.

When I go to the doctor ...

Spelling Pattern *ur*

Listen and write. Then check your answers.

1 f______ 2 c______ 3 s______ 4 t______ 5 p______

Now find more words with *ur* in the reading.

A Read. Then write the main idea and two details.

Getting a Cast

A broken arm can be scary. But don't worry! Doctors and nurses know what to do. First, they take an X-ray. That way, they can see inside your body. They check where the bone is broken. Then, they put a cast on your arm. After that, you have to wait. A broken arm takes about six to eight weeks to heal.

Main Idea	Detail
	Detail

The **main idea** is the big idea. It says what the reading is about. The main idea gives us the most important information.

The **details** are the smaller pieces of information. They help us understand the main idea. Details are sometimes called supporting ideas.

B Think and discuss. Look at the reading on the next page. Look at the title and the pictures. What do you think the main idea is?

I think it's about ...

C How does it feel when you discover something or solve a problem? Do a Think, Pair, Share.

It feels good to ...

Now read **A Surprise Cure**

Fiction

A Surprise Cure

How do scientists and doctors find new medicines?

Words in Context

Find these words in the reading. What do you think they mean?

scientist bacteria laboratory mess
attack liquid penicillin

mold
mould

Mold is a fungus. Mushrooms and yeast in bread are both types of fungi.

Aha, he sees the mold!
That's funny. There's mold growing on the dishes! How did it get here?
Check it out. We beat the bacteria!
Well done, mold!

Where are the bacteria?
That's a very good idea, Dr. Fleming!
Something in the mold was stopping them. Look, there's some liquid in the dish.
Mold juice! I need to find out more!

Dr. Fleming is a lucky man. Sometimes you find things when you aren't looking for them!
Aha! This is penicillium mold. I'm going to call the "mold juice" penicillin.
Penicillin kills bacteria. It can cure sick people. I have to make it a medicine. I have to share this discovery!
What other medicines do you know?
While the scientists were trying to make penicillin into medicine, they worked hard. They had to be sure it was safe.
Today, penicillin is one of the world's most important medicines. It has saved many, many lives. Some people say it has saved around 80 million lives so far!
PENICILLIN
PENICILLIN
And it all started because Dr. Fleming didn't clean up before he went on vacation!

Explore the Reading

A Complete the story map.

Characters
Who:

Setting
Where:
When:

Title

Problem
What was Fleming trying to do?

Solution
What happened when Fleming went on vacation?

B Think and write. What is the main idea of *A Surprise Cure*? What are some supporting details? Complete the graphic organizer.

Detail	Main Idea	Detail
Detail		Detail

C Think and discuss. What was Dr. Fleming's goal? How did he work toward it? What goal do you have? How do you work toward it?

Dr. Fleming's goal was ...

My goal is ...

What do we do when we're sick?

A Think and discuss. Complete the table.

When?	Where?	Problem	Treatment
			dead mouse medicine
20 BCE–400 CE			
		the plague	
		bacteria	

B We should do our best to stay healthy. What can we do? What can we eat or drink? Do a Numbered Heads Together routine.

C Think about your ideas from **B**. Make a list of the top three and share.

1 ______

2 ______

3 ______

We can ...

We should ...

My Reading Journal

Write three questions about illnesses or medicine. What do you want to know?

1 ______

2 ______

3 ______

Who do you think might find this unit interesting? Why?

______ might find it interesting because ______.

UNIT 10

Don't Push the Button

Question Starts

A Look at the picture. Then brainstorm questions. Write a list.

Who What Where

When Why How

B Look at your list from **A**. Which questions seem most interesting? Discuss them with the class.

Where does the big red glove come from?

How does the bird cage open?

C What new ideas or questions do you have now? Talk about your ideas with your partner.

What happens to the bird?

When does the ball fall?

D Think and discuss. What machines did you see on your way to school today?

E Think and discuss. Choose one of the machines you saw. Say one true thing about it. Then say what you think about it.

Now read **Moving Machines**

Nonfiction

Moving Machines

Parts of a Machine

Machines have lots of different moving parts. Looking at the inside of a clock can show you how many parts there are. There are four basic parts inside many of these machines—cranks, gears, levers, and pulleys.

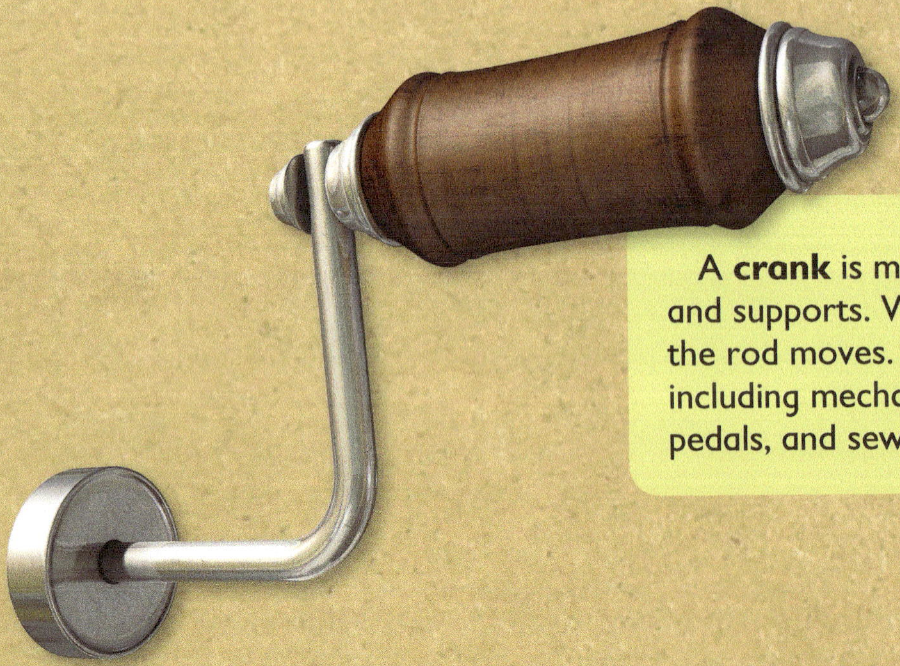

A **crank** is made from a handle, a thin rod, and supports. When you turn the handle, the rod moves. Many machines use cranks, including mechanical pencil sharpeners, bike pedals, and sewing machines.

Gears are like wheels with teeth. When the gears turn, the teeth connect to make them move. Gears can make something move faster or slower. Clocks, multi-speed bikes, and music boxes all use gears.

A **lever** is a strong, straight object that sits against a support. When either end of the lever is pushed down, the other side moves up. There are several types of levers. Scissors and seesaws are both examples of levers.

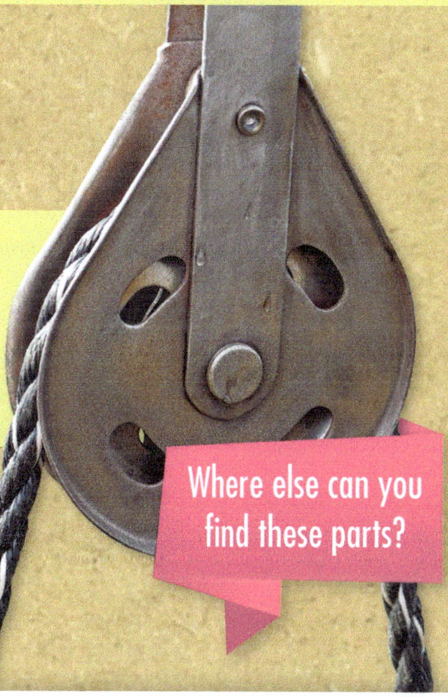

A **pulley** is a machine made from a wheel and a rope or chain. The rope or chain is pulled over the wheel and it helps lift heavy objects easily. Elevators and wells use pulleys.

Where else can you find these parts?

Words in Context

Find these words in the reading. What do you think they mean?

basic rod support either wind-up swan

Automata

Most machines only move when someone uses them, but automata can move on their own. In the past, automata were simpler. Some were even toys! Cuckoo clocks and wind-up dolls were popular automata before robots and automatic cleaning machines. People could turn a key or pull some strings and see the toys give a performance!

This robot cleans floors.

The designers were usually clock makers or inventors because they understood how the machines worked. Designers had to use their imaginations to make the machines look and move like real people or animals. It often took many people and a lot of hard work to build one.

Which of the four parts can you see?

This silver swan is at the Bowes Museum in England. It is made from many pieces of silver and gold. The river is made from glass rods. When someone turns the crank, the machine starts. The gears under the swan turn the glass rods, so it looks like moving water. Then, the swan turns its head and pulls a silver fish from the water. It even plays music.

Some automata need someone to press a button or put a coin in the machines to make them work. They can be very interesting to watch. There are automata in many places in our lives: in art museums, toy stores, and homes. These machines can be useful, fun, or both.

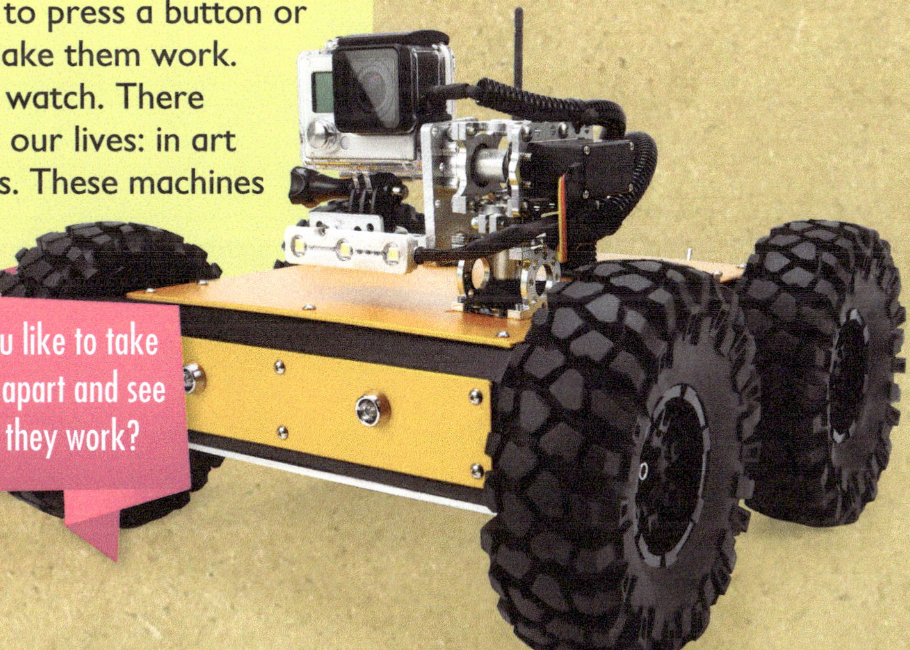

Do you like to take things apart and see how they work?

Explore the Reading

A Read and answer.

1 Which one has wheels with teeth?

2 Which one has a handle, a thin rod, and supports?

3 Which one is a strong, straight object that sits against a support?

4 Which one has a wheel and a rope or chain?

B Think and discuss. What parts can you see? How do you think it works?

C Think and discuss. Imagine you are building a machine. What would you like it to do?

My machine ...

A Read and choose. Then write *Fact* or *Opinion*.

[1]This automaton is a really cool toy. [2]It can play music. [3]It's made from metal. [4]It uses a lot of gears, some levers, and a crank. [5]All children want it.

1 Sentence 1 ________

2 Sentence 2 ________

3 Sentence 3 ________

4 Sentence 4 ________

5 Sentence 5 ________

A **fact** is a piece of information that is true. An **opinion** is what someone thinks. The words a writer uses can tell you if something is a fact or an opinion. An opinion often includes adjectives such as *perfect* or *useful* and verbs such as *think*, *believe*, or *like*.

B Read this text from *Searching for Sterling*. Underline the opinions.

"That was a hard day!" Ed shouted to the cowboys. "Time for some food!"

They were moving the cattle south. It was almost winter, but they were almost home.

"How's your new horse, Jules?" Ed asked his son.

"Oh, Sterling's great."

C Think and discuss. Look in your notebooks and find something you wrote. Where did you include facts and opinions?

I gave my opinion in ...

Now read **Searching for Sterling**

Fiction

Searching for Sterling

"That was a hard day!" Ed shouted to the cowboys. "Time for some food!"

What do you know about cowboys?

They were moving the cattle south. It was almost winter, but they were almost home.

"How's your new horse, Jules?" Ed asked his son.

"Oh, Sterling's great. When I push the Go to Sleep button, it shuts down," Jules explained.

"OK, you can laugh. But it's better than all your horses," he said. "You'll see."

Very early the next morning, Silas woke everyone up with his shouting. "Jules, come quickly! Sterling is gone!"

A big problem in a story is called **conflict**.

"Oh, no! Did I forget to shut it down last night? I have to find Sterling!" Jules decided to ask Sheriff Ada for help.

"Sterling isn't a normal horse, Sheriff," said Jules. "I need your motorcycle to catch it."

"Sure, you can borrow it," Sheriff Ada said. "To start and stop, you pull this lever."

Words in Context

Find these words in the reading. What do you think they mean?

cowboys cattle shuts down motorcycle fell asleep tough

WELCOME
SNOWMORE
POPULATION
357
SHERIFF
"But you have to bring it back tonight!" she shouted. "It's powerful. Be careful with it."
Jules loved the motorcycle. It was faster than Sterling! He drove it for kilometers through the desert. *I still have to look for Sterling*, he thought.
Jules was tired. He wanted to keep looking for Sterling, but it was too dark. He stopped to rest and fell asleep under the stars.
What do you think *under the stars* means?

Later that night, Jules awoke to a strange sound.

A coyote was eating all of his food! "Hey, get away from there!" Jules shouted.

Jules was upset. *I lost my horse, my food is gone, and it's getting cold. What a tough day!* he thought. *What do I do now?*

"The motorcycle! I promised to bring it back to the Sheriff yesterday!" He jumped on it and pulled the lever to turn it on. "Giddy-up!" Jules rode back to Snowmore as fast as he could.

He was very tired, very hungry, and very sad. *I'll never find Sterling*, he thought. Then, he saw Chayton outside the restaurant.

"Have you seen Sheriff Ada?" he asked.

"I haven't seen her today," Chayton said.

"I brought her motorcycle."

"Sheriff Ada! Sterling!"

"Good morning, Jules!"

"How did you find it?" Jules asked.

"It showed up here last night," said Sheriff Ada. "You pressed the Go Home button, not the Go to Sleep button!"

"You really are the best Sheriff in the West!" said Jules.

Explore the Reading

A Read and write *True* or *False*. Write the page where you found the answer.

1 The other cowboys like Jules's new horse. False 160

2 Silas didn't tell anyone that Sterling was gone. ______ ______

3 Jules fell asleep under the stars. ______ ______

4 Jules brought the motorcycle to the Sheriff on time. ______ ______

5 Sheriff Ada found Sterling. ______ ______

6 Jules pressed the Go to Sleep button. ______ ______

B Write one fact and one opinion.

1 Sterling

Fact: ______

Opinion: ______

2 The motorcycle

Fact: ______

Opinion: ______

3 The coyote

Fact: ______

Opinion: ______

C Think and discuss. Imagine you are Jules. Would you return the motorcycle to the Sheriff on time? Why or why not?

No, I would ...

I'd ...

Spelling Pattern *ough*

Listen and write. Then check your answers.

1 c______ 2 r______ 3 t______ 4 d______ 5 t______

Now find more words with *ough* in the reading.

Does technology make our lives easier?

A Think and write. What machines are there in the two readings? What does each one do?

Machine	What Does It Do?

B Think and discuss. What are three useful machines you use at home? Do a Round Robin.

I think the ...

I use ...

My Reading Journal

Which machine from this unit would you like to build? Who would you ask for help?

I'd like to build ____________ . I'd ask ____________ .

Which reading was your favorite in the whole book?

My favorite was ____________ .

Macmillan Education
4 Crinan Street
London N1 9XW
A division of Springer Nature Limited

Companies and representatives throughout the world

Literacy Book ISBN 978-1-786-32592-1
Student Book Pack ISBN 978-1-380-00235-8

Written by Katie Foufouti and Paul Mason

The authors have asserted their right to be identified as the authors of this work in accordance with the Copyright, Designs and Patents Act 1988.

First published 2019

Designed by Pronk Media, Inc.
Illustrated by Emiliano Ordás: pp. 4, 6, 139–142; Phil Corbett (Beehive Illustration): pp. 8–9; Barbara Cantini (Lemonade Illustration Agency): pp. 10–17, 31; Keri Green (Beehive Illustration): pp. 18–22, 41–42, 44, 47; Rob Foote (Beehive Illustration): pp. 31, 32–38, 47; Jennifer Zivoin (MB Artists): pp. 48–54, 61; Andre Ceolin (MB Artists): pp. 56–57; Jerome Basseur (Beehive Illustration): pp. 57, 59; Maine Diaz (MB Artists): pp. 62–69; Gustavo Mazali (Beehive Illustration): pp. 79–86; Marta Comito (Lemonade Illustration Agency): pp. 90–95; Guy Wolek (Blasco Agency): pp. 106–112, 125; Abigail dela Cruz (Lemonade Illustration Agency): pp. 125–133; Arpad Olbey (Beehive Illustration): pp. 144–150; Kevin Myers (Lemonade Illustration Agency): pp. 159–166.

Front cover design and concept by 3CD
Cover adaptation by Roberto Martinez
Cover illustration by Abigail dela Cruz (Lemonade Illustration Agency)
Cover photograph by Getty Images/Leonello Calvetti/Stocktrek Images (globe).
Picture research by Emily Taylor

Authors' acknowledgements
Katie Foufouti:
With special thanks to the Macmillan editors in Miami for their wonderful input. Dedicated to my late father, Dimitris.

Paul Mason:
I would like to acknowledge and thank the team at Macmillan and RedNova Learning. Working together was a privilege.

The publishers would like to thank: Viv Lambert and Mo Choy. Salwa Abid, Riham Almughrabi, Meryem Bennis, Leticia Blázquez, Angel Bonilla, Victor Cojulun, John Cruft, Silvia Díez de Rivera, Randa Farouk, Magda Giornazi, Vangelina Hernández, Quyen Ho, Ziad Jadallah, Youngkwang Jang, Faisal M'reish, Jackie Mustoe, Adriana Ochoa, Devrim Ozdemir, Maria Pia Ayala, Silvia Raya, Ola Refaat, Helen Sharbain, Sana Sifri, Esra Tosun, Lemmy Trujillo, Tamer Victor, Jake Whiddon, Sandra Wu, Amanda Zhang. Colegio Buckingham and Gabriela Rodríguez, Colegio Euterpe and Angélica Sánchez, Colegio Héroes Mexicanos and Marcelo Carlos Hernández Morales, Internaciones Campus Fraijanes and Ana Monica Thomas, New Victoria International College and Ghada Hassan Mokbel, The Southern Cross School and Dayana Acevedo, Antonia Lira, and Paula Jorquera, Verbo Quetzaltenango and Cindy Steicy Ixchiu Velásquez.

The authors and publishers would like to thank the following for permission to reproduce their photographs: **123RF**/Sergii Moskaliuk p. 98(flax); **Alamy**/Ilan Amihai p. 44(tl), Alamy/Dylan Becksholt p. 29(lynx), Alamy/Best View Stock pp. 43(tl), 47, Alamy/BibleLandPictures.com p. 43(br), Alamy/Chromorange/Lynne Otter p. 114(b), Alamy/Dinodia Photos p. 123(bcr), Alamy/Gary Doak pp. 101(tl) 102(br), Alamy/dpa picture alliance pp. 76(t), 77(cm), 78, Alamy/fStop Images p. 27(raccoons), Alamy/Richard Garvey-Williams p. 141, Alamy/Michael Hatfield p. 157(tr), Alamy/Thomas Kitchin p. 29(hare), Alamy/Daniel Krason p. 156(tr), 30(4), Alamy/Robert Landau p. 74(b), Alamy/Mauritius Images GmbH pp. 76(br), 77(tr), Alamy/Victor Nikitin pp. 28–29(background), 30(2), 31(background), Alamy/Brian Overcast p. 6, Alamy/Brian Peterson/Minneapolis Star Tribune p. 59(moore), Alamy/Martin Strmiska p. 123(br), Alamy/WENN Ltd p. 75(br), Alamy/Jeff Wheeler/Minneapolis Star Tribune p. 58(tr); Bluwave Creative/Luise Johnson-Dailey p. 40–41; **Getty Images**/AFP/Nicolas Asfouri p. 115(br), Getty Images/All Canada Photos p. 26–27(background), Getty Images/Alxpin p. 28(cm), Getty Images/Chel Beeson p. 88–89, Getty Images/Jim Bennett pp. 97, 99(cr), 102(tr), Getty Images/Leon Bennett p. 59(gray), Getty Images/Bestfotostudio p. 140(cucumbers), Getty Images/Matt Brown p. 58(bl), Getty Images/Stephen Clancy p. 117(cr), Getty Images/Jeffrey Coolidge p. 152–153, Getty Images/Corbis p. 138, Getty Images/C Squared Studios p. 156(bl), Getty Images/Cultura Exclusive/Ken Kiefer 2 pp. 120–121, Getty Images/Dazeley p. 140(gold), Getty Images/De Agostini p. 139(cr), Getty Images/Steve Debenport p. 143, Getty Images/Discovery Channel Images p. 117(tl), Getty Images/Dorling Kindersley pp. 100(spoon), 116(bl), Getty Images/Eureka_89 p. 116(tl), Getty Images/filo p. 59(t), Getty Images RF/fStop p. 77(book), Getty Images/gbrundin p. 115(bl), Getty Images/Kaanates p. 77(lettuce), Getty Images/T Kimura p. 31(tr), Getty Images/Jim Kruger p. 27(coyote), Getty Images/LDProd p. 45(br), Getty Images/Catherine MacBride p. 8–9, Getty Images/Marian pp. 98(bee), 99(bee), Getty Images/mg7 p. 101(bl), Getty Images/Mr_POKPAK p. 77(keys), Getty Images/Maksym Narodenko p. 140(peppers), Getty Images/National Geographic/Pete Ryan pp. 24–25, Getty Images/Maciej Noskowski pp. 26(b), 30(1), Getty Images/David Pedre pp. 136–137, Getty Images/Perspectives p. 122(cr), Getty Images/Plherrera pp. 58–59(background), Getty Images/Tim Robberts p. 45(t), Getty Images/David Sherman/NBAE p. 59(whalen), Getty Images/Jordan Siemens p. 116(tr), Getty Images/Twilightproductions pp. 157(br), 118(br), Getty Images/Vitalina p. 100(b), Getty Images/VitalyEdush pp. 122–123(background), Getty Images/WaterFrame RM p. 123(tr), Getty Images/wissanu01 p. 117(br), Getty Images/Alena Yakusheva p. 74(tr); **Rex Features**/Tina Norris/Shutterstock p. 101(br), Rex Features/TS/Keystone USA/Shutterstock p. 75(tl); **Shutterstock**/Africa Studio p. 116(blanket), Shutterstock/ArCaLu pp. 27(bears), 30(3), Shutterstock/Paolo Arsie Pelanda pp. 72–73, Shutterstock/avd p. 155(pulley), Shutterstock/Menno Boermans /Aurora Photos pp. 104–105, Shutterstock/Yuriy Boyko p. 43(chinese coin), Shutterstock/Orhan Cam p. 27(deer), Shutterstock/Chayanit p. 116(Rucksack), Shutterstock/Michael Conrad p. 27(squirrel), Shutterstock/Corund p. 155(lever), Shutterstock/Tony Craddock p. 113(tr), Shutterstock/Nick Cunard/REX p100(t), Shutterstock/Deepspacedave p. 115(tl), Shutterstock/FineShine p. 154(clock), Shutterstock/Jeabsam p. 77(coconut), Shutterstock/KMNPhoto p. 28(b), Shutterstock/Johannes Kornelius p. 139(tr), Shutterstock/Manfredxy p. 99(bl), Shutterstock/Terrence Meehan p. 159, Shutterstock/Serge Ostroverhoff p. 18–21(background), Shutterstock/Martin Pelanek p. 29(owl), Shutterstock/Photo Works p. 59(parker), Shutterstock/Andy Piatt p. 116(walkie talkie), Shutterstock/Ragnarock pp. 42–43(background), 44–45(background), Shutterstock/Shiyan Sergiy p. 154(crank), Shutterstock/Vladyslav Starozhylov p. 158, Shutterstock/Taigi pp. 4–5(background), 6–7(background), 23(background), 39(background), 55(background), 71(background), 87(background), 119(background), 135(background), 103(background), 151(background), 167(background), Shutterstock/Wavebreakmedia p. 155(cogs), Shutterstock/Xinhua/REX pp. 114(tr), 118(tr).

Commissioned photographs by: Luise Johnson-Dailey, Bluwave Creative pp. 40–41

Printed and bound in Uruguay

2023
30